Digital Content Management
Complete Self-Assessment Guide

The guidance in this Self-Assessment is based on Digital Content Management best practices and standards in business process architecture, design and quality management. The guidance is also based on the professional judgment of the individual collaborators listed in the Acknowledgments.

Table of Contents

About The Art of Service

The Art of Service, Business Process Architects since 2000, is dedicated to helping stakeholders achieve excellence.

Defining, designing, creating, and implementing a process to solve a stakeholders challenge or meet an objective is the most valuable role… In EVERY group, company, organization and department.

Unless you're talking a one-time, single-use project, there should be a process. Whether that process is managed and implemented by humans, AI, or a combination of the two, it needs to be designed by someone with a complex enough perspective to ask the right questions.

Someone capable of asking the right questions and step back and say, 'What are we really trying to accomplish here? And is there a different way to look at it?'

With The Art of Service's Standard Requirements Self-Assessments, we empower people who can do just that — whether their title is marketer, entrepreneur, manager, salesperson, consultant, Business Process Manager, executive assistant, IT Manager, CIO etc... —they are the people who rule the future. They are people who watch the process as it happens, and ask the right questions to make the process work better.

Contact us when you need any support with this Self-Assessment and any help with templates, blue-prints and examples of standard documents you might need:

http://theartofservice.com
service@theartofservice.com

Included Resources - how to access

Included with your purchase of the book is the Digital Content

Management Self-Assessment Spreadsheet Dashboard which contains all questions and Self-Assessment areas and auto-generates insights, graphs, and project RACI planning - all with examples to get you started right away.

How? Simply send an email to
access@theartofservice.com
with this books' title in the subject to get the Digital Content Management Self Assessment Tool right away.

You will receive the following contents with New and Updated specific criteria:

- The latest quick edition of the book in PDF

- The latest complete edition of the book in PDF, which criteria correspond to the criteria in...

- The Self-Assessment Excel Dashboard, and...

- Example pre-filled Self-Assessment Excel Dashboard to get familiar with results generation

- In-depth specific Checklists covering the topic

- Project management checklists and templates to assist with implementation

Purpose of this Self-Assessment

This Self-Assessment has been developed to improve understanding of the requirements and elements of Digital Content Management, based on best practices and standards in business process architecture, design and quality management.

It is designed to allow for a rapid Self-Assessment to determine how closely existing management practices and procedures correspond to the elements of the Self-Assessment.

The criteria of requirements and elements of Digital Content Management have been rephrased in the format of a Self-Assessment questionnaire, with a seven-criterion scoring system, as explained in this document.

In this format, even with limited background knowledge of Digital Content Management, a manager can quickly review existing operations to determine how they measure up to the standards. This in turn can serve as the starting point of a 'gap analysis' to identify management tools or system elements that might usefully be implemented in the organization to help improve overall performance.

How to use the Self-Assessment

On the following pages are a series of questions to identify to what extent your Digital Content Management initiative is complete in comparison to the requirements set in standards.

To facilitate answering the questions, there is a space in front of each question to enter a score on a scale of '1' to '5'.

1 Strongly Disagree

2 Disagree

3 Neutral

4 Agree

5 Strongly Agree

Read the question and rate it with the following in front of mind:

'In my belief,
the answer to this question is clearly defined'.

There are two ways in which you can choose to interpret this statement;
1. how aware are you that the answer to the question is clearly defined
2. for more in-depth analysis you can choose to gather evidence and confirm the answer to the question. This obviously will take more time, most Self-Assessment users opt for the first way to interpret the question and dig deeper later on based on the outcome of the overall Self-Assessment.

A score of '1' would mean that the answer is not clear at all, where a '5' would mean the answer is crystal clear and defined. Leave emtpy when the question is not applicable or you don't want to answer it, you can skip it without affecting your score. Write your score in the space provided.

After you have responded to all the appropriate statements in each section, compute your average score for that section, using the formula provided, and round to the nearest tenth. Then transfer to the corresponding spoke in the Digital Content Management Scorecard on the second next page of the Self-Assessment.

Your completed Digital Content Management Scorecard will give you a clear presentation of which Digital Content Management areas need attention.

Digital Content Management Scorecard Example

Example of how the finalized Scorecard can look like:

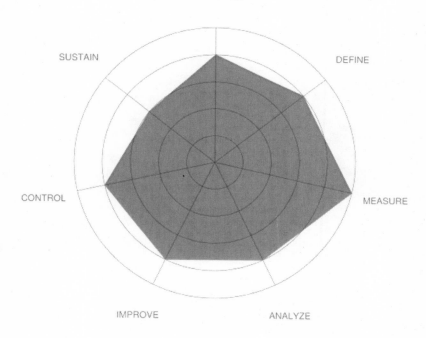

Digital Content Management Scorecard

Your Scores:

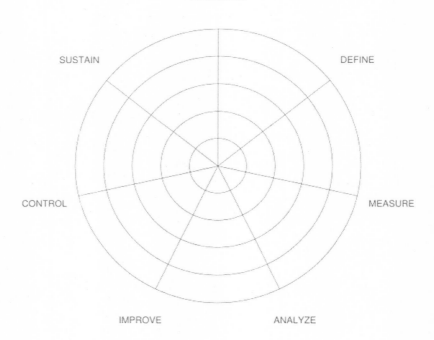

BEGINNING OF THE SELF-ASSESSMENT:

CRITERION #1: RECOGNIZE

INTENT: Be aware of the need for change. Recognize that there is an unfavorable variation, problem or symptom.

In my belief, the answer to this question is clearly defined:

5 Strongly Agree

4 Agree

3 Neutral

2 Disagree

1 Strongly Disagree

1. What is the extent or complexity of the Digital Content Management problem?
<--- Score

2. What Digital Content Management events should you attend?
<--- Score

3. Who else hopes to benefit from it?

<--- Score

4. What are the expected benefits of Digital Content Management to the stakeholder?
<--- Score

5. What situation(s) led to this Digital Content Management Self Assessment?
<--- Score

6. Who defines the rules in relation to any given issue?
<--- Score

7. What tools and technologies are needed for a custom Digital Content Management project?
<--- Score

8. Do you need to avoid or amend any Digital Content Management activities?
<--- Score

9. Are there any specific expectations or concerns about the Digital Content Management team, Digital Content Management itself?
<--- Score

10. Can management personnel recognize the monetary benefit of Digital Content Management?
<--- Score

11. What are the Digital Content Management resources needed?
<--- Score

12. Will new equipment/products be required to facilitate Digital Content Management delivery, for

example is new software needed?
<--- Score

13. What activities does the governance board need to consider?
<--- Score

14. To what extent does each concerned units management team recognize Digital Content Management as an effective investment?
<--- Score

15. What do you need to start doing?
<--- Score

16. How much are sponsors, customers, partners, stakeholders involved in Digital Content Management? In other words, what are the risks, if Digital Content Management does not deliver successfully?
<--- Score

17. What is the problem or issue?
<--- Score

18. What types of annotations need to be migrated?
<--- Score

19. How can auditing be a preventative security measure?
<--- Score

20. Will a response program recognize when a crisis occurs and provide some level of response?
<--- Score

21. Are controls defined to recognize and contain problems?
<--- Score

22. Does your organization need more Digital Content Management education?
<--- Score

23. Why is this needed?
<--- Score

24. What resources or support might you need?
<--- Score

25. Will Digital Content Management deliverables need to be tested and, if so, by whom?
<--- Score

26. Does Digital Content Management create potential expectations in other areas that need to be recognized and considered?
<--- Score

27. What training and capacity building actions are needed to implement proposed reforms?
<--- Score

28. Who are your key stakeholders who need to sign off?
<--- Score

29. Do you know what you need to know about Digital Content Management?
<--- Score

30. What should be considered when identifying available resources, constraints, and deadlines?
<--- Score

31. Who should resolve the Digital Content Management issues?
<--- Score

32. How are training requirements identified?
<--- Score

33. How do software as a service (SaaS) vendors handle the sourcing issue?
<--- Score

34. What Digital Content Management capabilities do you need?
<--- Score

35. As a sponsor, customer or management, how important is it to meet goals, objectives?
<--- Score

36. What are the timeframes required to resolve each of the issues/problems?
<--- Score

37. What do you need to capture and manage your digital content?
<--- Score

38. What does Digital Content Management success mean to the stakeholders?
<--- Score

39. Which needs are not included or involved?

<--- Score

40. Have you identified your Digital Content Management key performance indicators?
<--- Score

41. How are you going to measure success?
<--- Score

42. What Digital Content Management coordination do you need?
<--- Score

43. Are you dealing with any of the same issues today as yesterday? What can you do about this?
<--- Score

44. How many trainings, in total, are needed?
<--- Score

45. For your Digital Content Management project, identify and describe the business environment, is there more than one layer to the business environment?
<--- Score

46. Are there any revenue recognition issues?
<--- Score

47. What is needed for longer term management of the digital content?
<--- Score

48. What Digital Content Management problem should be solved?
<--- Score

49. Is it clear when you think of the day ahead of you what activities and tasks you need to complete?
<--- Score

50. What are the minority interests and what amount of minority interests can be recognized?
<--- Score

51. Who needs to know about Digital Content Management?
<--- Score

52. Who needs budgets?
<--- Score

53. Is the need for organizational change recognized?
<--- Score

54. Whom do you really need or want to serve?
<--- Score

55. What is the Digital Content Management problem definition? What do you need to resolve?
<--- Score

56. Where do you need to exercise leadership?
<--- Score

57. What do employees need in the short term?
<--- Score

58. Is it needed?
<--- Score

59. To what extent would your organization benefit

from being recognized as a award recipient?
<--- Score

60. Did you miss any major Digital Content Management issues?
<--- Score

61. How do you recognize an Digital Content Management objection?
<--- Score

62. What are the clients issues and concerns?
<--- Score

63. How do you take a forward-looking perspective in identifying Digital Content Management research related to market response and models?
<--- Score

64. Are there any known issues/bugs in the system?
<--- Score

65. How are the Digital Content Management's objectives aligned to the group's overall stakeholder strategy?
<--- Score

66. What is the problem and/or vulnerability?
<--- Score

67. What needs to stay?
<--- Score

68. What is the smallest subset of the problem you can usefully solve?

<--- Score

69. What vendors make products that address the Digital Content Management needs?
<--- Score

70. Why the need?
<--- Score

71. What problems are you facing and how do you consider Digital Content Management will circumvent those obstacles?
<--- Score

72. Are losses recognized in a timely manner?
<--- Score

73. Envisioned future: what capabilities are wanted and needed the most?
<--- Score

74. Do you have/need 24-hour access to key personnel?
<--- Score

75. Are there Digital Content Management problems defined?
<--- Score

76. Who needs to know?
<--- Score

77. What else needs to be measured?
<--- Score

78. What would happen if Digital Content

Management weren't done?
<--- Score

79. Are employees recognized or rewarded for performance that demonstrates the highest levels of integrity?
<--- Score

80. How do you identify the kinds of information that you will need?
<--- Score

81. What extra resources will you need?
<--- Score

82. Do you need different information or graphics?
<--- Score

83. Which issues are too important to ignore?
<--- Score

84. Is the quality assurance team identified?
<--- Score

85. How do you assess your Digital Content Management workforce capability and capacity needs, including skills, competencies, and staffing levels?
<--- Score

86. Will it solve real problems?
<--- Score

87. Does the problem have ethical dimensions?
<--- Score

88. Are problem definition and motivation clearly presented?
<--- Score

89. What will the customer satisfaction entail, that is, what are the needs you are trying to meet?
<--- Score

90. How do you identify subcontractor relationships?
<--- Score

91. What are the stakeholder objectives to be achieved with Digital Content Management?
<--- Score

92. Which information does the Digital Content Management business case need to include?
<--- Score

93. What creative shifts do you need to take?
<--- Score

94. What is the recognized need?
<--- Score

95. How do you recognize an objection?
<--- Score

96. Are your goals realistic? Do you need to redefine your problem? Perhaps the problem has changed or maybe you have reached your goal and need to set a new one?
<--- Score

97. Who needs what information?
<--- Score

98. Are there regulatory / compliance issues?
<--- Score

99. Would you recognize a threat from the inside?
<--- Score

100. When a Digital Content Management manager recognizes a problem, what options are available?
<--- Score

101. How does it fit into your organizational needs and tasks?
<--- Score

102. Consider your own Digital Content Management project, what types of organizational problems do you think might be causing or affecting your problem, based on the work done so far?
<--- Score

Add up total points for this section:
_ _ _ _ _ = Total points for this section

Divided by: _ _ _ _ _ _ (number of statements answered) = _ _ _ _ _ _
Average score for this section

Transfer your score to the Digital Content Management Index at the beginning of the Self-Assessment.

CRITERION #2: DEFINE:

INTENT: Formulate the stakeholder problem. Define the problem, needs and objectives.

In my belief, the answer to this question is clearly defined:

5 Strongly Agree

4 Agree

3 Neutral

2 Disagree

1 Strongly Disagree

1. Are required metrics defined, what are they?
<--- Score

2. Are approval levels defined for contracts and supplements to contracts?
<--- Score

3. Are improvement team members fully trained on Digital Content Management?

<--- Score

4. How do you gather requirements?
<--- Score

5. Has a Digital Content Management requirement not been met?
<--- Score

6. Have all of the relationships been defined properly?
<--- Score

7. Do the problem and goal statements meet the SMART criteria (specific, measurable, attainable, relevant, and time-bound)?
<--- Score

8. Is scope creep really all bad news?
<--- Score

9. Are all requirements met?
<--- Score

10. What specifically is the problem? Where does it occur? When does it occur? What is its extent?
<--- Score

11. How was the 'as is' process map developed, reviewed, verified and validated?
<--- Score

12. What is the scope of the Digital Content Management work?
<--- Score

13. Has everyone on the team, including the team

leaders, been properly trained?
<--- Score

14. Is there a critical path to deliver Digital Content Management results?
<--- Score

15. What is the definition of success?
<--- Score

16. What are the dynamics of the communication plan?
<--- Score

17. What would be the goal or target for a Digital Content Management's improvement team?
<--- Score

18. Has/have the customer(s) been identified?
<--- Score

19. How do you think the partners involved in Digital Content Management would have defined success?
<--- Score

20. Are task requirements clearly defined?
<--- Score

21. What is in the scope and what is not in scope?
<--- Score

22. Are team charters developed?
<--- Score

23. Do you have a Digital Content Management success story or case study ready to tell and share?

<--- Score

24. Is the team formed and are team leaders (Coaches and Management Leads) assigned?
<--- Score

25. Will team members regularly document their Digital Content Management work?
<--- Score

26. Are agreements required?
<--- Score

27. How often are the team meetings?
<--- Score

28. How did the Digital Content Management manager receive input to the development of a Digital Content Management improvement plan and the estimated completion dates/times of each activity?
<--- Score

29. Who is gathering Digital Content Management information?
<--- Score

30. What are the boundaries of the scope? What is in bounds and what is not? What is the start point? What is the stop point?
<--- Score

31. Is Digital Content Management currently on schedule according to the plan?
<--- Score

32. How would you define the culture at your organization, how susceptible is it to Digital Content Management changes?
<--- Score

33. Is special Digital Content Management user knowledge required?
<--- Score

34. How is the team tracking and documenting its work?
<--- Score

35. Is there regularly 100% attendance at the team meetings? If not, have appointed substitutes attended to preserve cross-functionality and full representation?
<--- Score

36. Does the team have regular meetings?
<--- Score

37. What sources do you use to gather information for a Digital Content Management study?
<--- Score

38. Is the team sponsored by a champion or stakeholder leader?
<--- Score

39. Is the current 'as is' process being followed? If not, what are the discrepancies?
<--- Score

40. Is the team adequately staffed with the desired cross-functionality? If not, what additional resources

are available to the team?
<--- Score

41. Is the Digital Content Management scope manageable?
<--- Score

42. Have the customer needs been translated into specific, measurable requirements? How?
<--- Score

43. Is there any additional Digital Content Management definition of success?
<--- Score

44. How do you gather Digital Content Management requirements?
<--- Score

45. Is the scope of Digital Content Management defined?
<--- Score

46. Why are you doing Digital Content Management and what is the scope?
<--- Score

47. What is a worst-case scenario for losses?
<--- Score

48. What is the worst case scenario?
<--- Score

49. What are the compelling stakeholder reasons for embarking on Digital Content Management?
<--- Score

50. How will variation in the actual durations of each activity be dealt with to ensure that the expected Digital Content Management results are met?
<--- Score

51. Are there any constraints known that bear on the ability to perform Digital Content Management work? How is the team addressing them?
<--- Score

52. What sort of initial information to gather?
<--- Score

53. How do you build the right business case?
<--- Score

54. How do you gather the stories?
<--- Score

55. How can the value of Digital Content Management be defined?
<--- Score

56. Is there a completed SIPOC representation, describing the Suppliers, Inputs, Process, Outputs, and Customers?
<--- Score

57. What scope do you want your strategy to cover?
<--- Score

58. Has the improvement team collected the 'voice of the customer' (obtained feedback – qualitative and quantitative)?
<--- Score

59. How would you define Digital Content Management leadership?
<--- Score

60. Has the Digital Content Management work been fairly and/or equitably divided and delegated among team members who are qualified and capable to perform the work? Has everyone contributed?
<--- Score

61. Has a team charter been developed and communicated?
<--- Score

62. What is the scope of Digital Content Management?
<--- Score

63. Is the team equipped with available and reliable resources?
<--- Score

64. Has anyone else (internal or external to the group) attempted to solve this problem or a similar one before? If so, what knowledge can be leveraged from these previous efforts?
<--- Score

65. What information do you gather?
<--- Score

66. Who is gathering information?
<--- Score

67. Is Digital Content Management linked to key stakeholder goals and objectives?

<--- Score

68. How do you catch Digital Content Management definition inconsistencies?
<--- Score

69. What Digital Content Management services do you require?
<--- Score

70. Is Digital Content Management required?
<--- Score

71. Are there different segments of customers?
<--- Score

72. Have specific policy objectives been defined?
<--- Score

73. Who approved the Digital Content Management scope?
<--- Score

74. What was the context?
<--- Score

75. Who are the Digital Content Management improvement team members, including Management Leads and Coaches?
<--- Score

76. What customer feedback methods were used to solicit their input?
<--- Score

77. Is the Digital Content Management scope

complete and appropriately sized?
<--- Score

78. Is a fully trained team formed, supported, and committed to work on the Digital Content Management improvements?
<--- Score

79. What is the scope of the Digital Content Management effort?
<--- Score

80. What are the Digital Content Management use cases?
<--- Score

81. Scope of sensitive information?
<--- Score

82. What is in scope?
<--- Score

83. What critical content must be communicated – who, what, when, where, and how?
<--- Score

84. How are consistent Digital Content Management definitions important?
<--- Score

85. What baselines are required to be defined and managed?
<--- Score

86. If substitutes have been appointed, have they been briefed on the Digital Content Management

goals and received regular communications as to the progress to date?

<--- Score

87. What knowledge or experience is required?

<--- Score

88. What constraints exist that might impact the team?

<--- Score

89. Are customers identified and high impact areas defined?

<--- Score

90. How will the Digital Content Management team and the group measure complete success of Digital Content Management?

<--- Score

91. What is out-of-scope initially?

<--- Score

92. How does the Digital Content Management manager ensure against scope creep?

<--- Score

93. Has a high-level 'as is' process map been completed, verified and validated?

<--- Score

94. Will a Digital Content Management production readiness review be required?

<--- Score

95. What are the requirements for audit information?

<--- Score

96. What are the rough order estimates on cost savings/opportunities that Digital Content Management brings?
<--- Score

97. The political context: who holds power?
<--- Score

98. Will team members perform Digital Content Management work when assigned and in a timely fashion?
<--- Score

99. What key stakeholder process output measure(s) does Digital Content Management leverage and how?
<--- Score

100. Has your scope been defined?
<--- Score

101. What information should you gather?
<--- Score

102. What intelligence can you gather?
<--- Score

103. What are the Roles and Responsibilities for each team member and its leadership? Where is this documented?
<--- Score

104. How do you hand over Digital Content Management context?
<--- Score

105. What is the context?
<--- Score

106. How do you manage unclear Digital Content Management requirements?
<--- Score

107. When is the estimated completion date?
<--- Score

108. What is out of scope?
<--- Score

109. Is the improvement team aware of the different versions of a process: what they think it is vs. what it actually is vs. what it should be vs. what it could be?
<--- Score

110. Is the work to date meeting requirements?
<--- Score

111. How do you keep key subject matter experts in the loop?
<--- Score

112. Are stakeholder processes mapped?
<--- Score

113. What system do you use for gathering Digital Content Management information?
<--- Score

114. Has the direction changed at all during the course of Digital Content Management? If so, when did it change and why?

<--- Score

115. Is there a completed, verified, and validated high-level 'as is' (not 'should be' or 'could be') stakeholder process map?
<--- Score

116. Are customer(s) identified and segmented according to their different needs and requirements?
<--- Score

117. What are the tasks and definitions?
<--- Score

118. What are the core elements of the Digital Content Management business case?
<--- Score

119. Are roles and responsibilities formally defined?
<--- Score

120. Is there a Digital Content Management management charter, including stakeholder case, problem and goal statements, scope, milestones, roles and responsibilities, communication plan?
<--- Score

121. Where can you gather more information?
<--- Score

122. Are the Digital Content Management requirements testable?
<--- Score

123. Are audit criteria, scope, frequency and methods defined?

<--- Score

124. Are different versions of process maps needed to account for the different types of inputs?
<--- Score

125. When is/was the Digital Content Management start date?
<--- Score

126. What defines best in class?
<--- Score

127. When are meeting minutes sent out? Who is on the distribution list?
<--- Score

128. Is data collected and displayed to better understand customer(s) critical needs and requirements.
<--- Score

129. Are the Digital Content Management requirements complete?
<--- Score

130. Is full participation by members in regularly held team meetings guaranteed?
<--- Score

131. How do you manage changes in Digital Content Management requirements?
<--- Score

132. Has a project plan, Gantt chart, or similar been developed/completed?

<--- Score

133. Is it clearly defined in and to your organization what you do?
<--- Score

Add up total points for this section:
_____ = Total points for this section

Divided by: _____ (number of statements answered) = _____
Average score for this section

Transfer your score to the Digital Content Management Index at the beginning of the Self-Assessment.

CRITERION #3: MEASURE:

INTENT: Gather the correct data. Measure the current performance and evolution of the situation.

In my belief, the answer to this question is clearly defined:

5 Strongly Agree

4 Agree

3 Neutral

2 Disagree

1 Strongly Disagree

1. How do you control the overall costs of your work processes?
<--- Score

2. Are the units of measure consistent?
<--- Score

3. How do your measurements capture actionable Digital Content Management information for use in

exceeding your customers expectations and securing your customers engagement?

<--- Score

4. What are predictive Digital Content Management analytics?

<--- Score

5. What is the cost of rework?

<--- Score

6. What is measured? Why?

<--- Score

7. Is it possible to estimate the impact of unanticipated complexity such as wrong or failed assumptions, feedback, etcetera on proposed reforms?

<--- Score

8. Does the Digital Content Management task fit the client's priorities?

<--- Score

9. What could cause you to change course?

<--- Score

10. What does verifying compliance entail?

<--- Score

11. How will you measure your Digital Content Management effectiveness?

<--- Score

12. What does losing customers cost your organization?

<--- Score

13. How do you stay flexible and focused to recognize larger Digital Content Management results?
<--- Score

14. Which measures and indicators matter?
<--- Score

15. Have design-to-cost goals been established?
<--- Score

16. What are the uncertainties surrounding estimates of impact?
<--- Score

17. Who pays the cost?
<--- Score

18. Are you aware of what could cause a problem?
<--- Score

19. What are the costs of delaying Digital Content Management action?
<--- Score

20. How do you verify and develop ideas and innovations?
<--- Score

21. How is performance measured?
<--- Score

22. Is the solution cost-effective?
<--- Score

23. What is the Digital Content Management business impact?
<--- Score

24. What measurements are being captured?
<--- Score

25. How long to keep data and how to manage retention costs?
<--- Score

26. What is the total fixed cost?
<--- Score

27. What is an unallowable cost?
<--- Score

28. Are you able to realize any cost savings?
<--- Score

29. How do you measure efficient delivery of Digital Content Management services?
<--- Score

30. How do you prevent mis-estimating cost?
<--- Score

31. What are your primary costs, revenues, assets?
<--- Score

32. Is a follow-up focused external Digital Content Management review required?
<--- Score

33. How do you verify performance?
<--- Score

34. How do you verify and validate the Digital Content Management data?
<--- Score

35. How frequently do you track Digital Content Management measures?
<--- Score

36. What are the costs?
<--- Score

37. How will you measure success?
<--- Score

38. Why do the measurements/indicators matter?
<--- Score

39. What are the costs and benefits?
<--- Score

40. How can you manage cost down?
<--- Score

41. How will costs be allocated?
<--- Score

42. How is the value delivered by Digital Content Management being measured?
<--- Score

43. How are you verifying it?
<--- Score

44. How do you verify the authenticity of the data and information used?

<--- Score

45. How will success or failure be measured?
<--- Score

46. At what cost?
<--- Score

47. Where can you go to verify the info?
<--- Score

48. Do you have a flow diagram of what happens?
<--- Score

49. How are measurements made?
<--- Score

50. What methods are feasible and acceptable to estimate the impact of reforms?
<--- Score

51. Did you tackle the cause or the symptom?
<--- Score

52. Among the Digital Content Management product and service cost to be estimated, which is considered hardest to estimate?
<--- Score

53. What measurements are possible, practicable and meaningful?
<--- Score

54. How do you measure success?
<--- Score

55. How do you measure variability?
<--- Score

56. Are you taking your company in the direction of better and revenue or cheaper and cost?
<--- Score

57. How will effects be measured?
<--- Score

58. How will measures be used to manage and adapt?
<--- Score

59. Are the measurements objective?
<--- Score

60. What could cause delays in the schedule?
<--- Score

61. What causes extra work or rework?
<--- Score

62. What users will be impacted?
<--- Score

63. Do you aggressively reward and promote the people who have the biggest impact on creating excellent Digital Content Management services/ products?
<--- Score

64. What are you verifying?
<--- Score

65. What harm might be caused?
<--- Score

66. How can you reduce costs?
<--- Score

67. Has a cost center been established?
<--- Score

68. What can be used to verify compliance?
<--- Score

69. Have you made assumptions about the shape of the future, particularly its impact on your customers and competitors?
<--- Score

70. What are the Digital Content Management key cost drivers?
<--- Score

71. What are hidden Digital Content Management quality costs?
<--- Score

72. How are costs allocated?
<--- Score

73. How do you measure lifecycle phases?
<--- Score

74. Was a business case (cost/benefit) developed?
<--- Score

75. What is the cause of any Digital Content Management gaps?
<--- Score

76. Why do you expend time and effort to implement measurement, for whom?
<--- Score

77. What is your Digital Content Management quality cost segregation study?
<--- Score

78. Are there any easy-to-implement alternatives to Digital Content Management? Sometimes other solutions are available that do not require the cost implications of a full-blown project?
<--- Score

79. What disadvantage does this cause for the user?
<--- Score

80. What is the total cost related to deploying Digital Content Management, including any consulting or professional services?
<--- Score

81. What do people want to verify?
<--- Score

82. What drives O&M cost?
<--- Score

83. Does a Digital Content Management quantification method exist?
<--- Score

84. How sensitive must the Digital Content Management strategy be to cost?
<--- Score

85. Are indirect costs charged to the Digital Content Management program?
<--- Score

86. What are your operating costs?
<--- Score

87. How can you measure Digital Content Management in a systematic way?
<--- Score

88. What potential environmental factors impact the Digital Content Management effort?
<--- Score

89. Are Digital Content Management vulnerabilities categorized and prioritized?
<--- Score

90. Which Digital Content Management impacts are significant?
<--- Score

91. How can you reduce the costs of obtaining inputs?
<--- Score

92. What are the strategic priorities for this year?
<--- Score

93. How much does it cost?
<--- Score

94. Are missed Digital Content Management opportunities costing your organization money?
<--- Score

95. What are the estimated costs of proposed changes?
<--- Score

96. How frequently do you verify your Digital Content Management strategy?
<--- Score

97. Where is it measured?
<--- Score

98. Do you verify that corrective actions were taken?
<--- Score

99. What details are required of the Digital Content Management cost structure?
<--- Score

100. What does your operating model cost?
<--- Score

101. Are there measurements based on task performance?
<--- Score

102. Is the cost worth the Digital Content Management effort ?
<--- Score

103. What would be a real cause for concern?
<--- Score

104. Why a Digital Content Management focus?
<--- Score

105. Was a life-cycle cost analysis performed?

<--- Score

106. Are there competing Digital Content Management priorities?
<--- Score

107. What is your decision requirements diagram?
<--- Score

108. Who is involved in verifying compliance?
<--- Score

109. What are the current costs of the Digital Content Management process?
<--- Score

110. How do you verify Digital Content Management completeness and accuracy?
<--- Score

111. Who should receive measurement reports?
<--- Score

112. Does management have the right priorities among projects?
<--- Score

113. How do you verify the Digital Content Management requirements quality?
<--- Score

114. The approach of traditional Digital Content Management works for detail complexity but is focused on a systematic approach rather than an understanding of the nature of systems themselves, what approach will permit your organization to deal

with the kind of unpredictable emergent behaviors that dynamic complexity can introduce?
<--- Score

115. Is there an opportunity to verify requirements?
<--- Score

116. How can you measure the performance?
<--- Score

117. What tests verify requirements?
<--- Score

118. Are the Digital Content Management benefits worth its costs?
<--- Score

119. Do you effectively measure and reward individual and team performance?
<--- Score

120. Do you have an issue in getting priority?
<--- Score

121. Is the scope of Digital Content Management cost analysis cost-effective?
<--- Score

122. What are allowable costs?
<--- Score

123. Do the benefits outweigh the costs?
<--- Score

124. What are your customers expectations and measures?

<--- Score

125. When should you bother with diagrams?
<--- Score

126. What relevant entities could be measured?
<--- Score

127. What causes innovation to fail or succeed in your organization?
<--- Score

128. How is progress measured?
<--- Score

129. Will Digital Content Management have an impact on current business continuity, disaster recovery processes and/or infrastructure?
<--- Score

130. Are supply costs steady or fluctuating?
<--- Score

131. What are the costs of reform?
<--- Score

132. How do you aggregate measures across priorities?
<--- Score

133. When are costs are incurred?
<--- Score

134. What is the root cause(s) of the problem?
<--- Score

Add up total points for this section:
_____ = Total points for this section

Divided by: _____ (number of
statements answered) = _____
Average score for this section

Transfer your score to the Digital
Content Management Index at the
beginning of the Self-Assessment.

CRITERION #4: ANALYZE:

INTENT: Analyze causes, assumptions and hypotheses.

In my belief, the answer to this question is clearly defined:

5 Strongly Agree

4 Agree

3 Neutral

2 Disagree

1 Strongly Disagree

1. What are your current levels and trends in key measures or indicators of Digital Content Management product and process performance that are important to and directly serve your customers? How do these results compare with the performance of your competitors and other organizations with similar offerings?
<--- Score

2. Has data output been validated?

<--- Score

3. What are the disruptive Digital Content Management technologies that enable your organization to radically change your business processes?
<--- Score

4. How many input/output points does it require?
<--- Score

5. Do several people in different organizational units assist with the Digital Content Management process?
<--- Score

6. Has an output goal been set?
<--- Score

7. What are the processes for audit reporting and management?
<--- Score

8. How was the detailed process map generated, verified, and validated?
<--- Score

9. What are the Digital Content Management design outputs?
<--- Score

10. Should you invest in industry-recognized qualifications?
<--- Score

11. What is your organizations process which leads to recognition of value generation?

<--- Score

12. What is the complexity of the output produced?
<--- Score

13. What are the Digital Content Management business drivers?
<--- Score

14. What did the team gain from developing a sub-process map?
<--- Score

15. Was a cause-and-effect diagram used to explore the different types of causes (or sources of variation)?
<--- Score

16. What output to create?
<--- Score

17. How good is the installation process?
<--- Score

18. What other jobs or tasks affect the performance of the steps in the Digital Content Management process?
<--- Score

19. What quality tools were used to get through the analyze phase?
<--- Score

20. How will corresponding data be collected?
<--- Score

21. How will the Digital Content Management data be captured?

<--- Score

22. Does the system have any data integrity check for a file?
<--- Score

23. What were the crucial 'moments of truth' on the process map?
<--- Score

24. What are the revised rough estimates of the financial savings/opportunity for Digital Content Management improvements?
<--- Score

25. What data do you need to collect?
<--- Score

26. Is the gap/opportunity displayed and communicated in financial terms?
<--- Score

27. What Digital Content Management data do you gather or use now?
<--- Score

28. How do you ensure that the Digital Content Management opportunity is realistic?
<--- Score

29. How do you use Digital Content Management data and information to support organizational decision making and innovation?
<--- Score

30. What data needs to be migrated?

<--- Score

31. What Digital Content Management metrics are outputs of the process?
<--- Score

32. What are the key elements of your Digital Content Management performance improvement system, including your evaluation, organizational learning, and innovation processes?
<--- Score

33. How much data needs to be migrated?
<--- Score

34. Is pre-qualification of suppliers carried out?
<--- Score

35. How often will data be collected for measures?
<--- Score

36. Is there a strict change management process?
<--- Score

37. What internal processes need improvement?
<--- Score

38. Do staff qualifications match your project?
<--- Score

39. Are all staff in core Digital Content Management subjects Highly Qualified?
<--- Score

40. What qualifications are needed?
<--- Score

41. Do your contracts/agreements contain data security obligations?
<--- Score

42. What are your Digital Content Management processes?
<--- Score

43. What are your key performance measures or indicators and in-process measures for the control and improvement of your Digital Content Management processes?
<--- Score

44. Who is involved in the management review process?
<--- Score

45. What kind of crime could a potential new hire have committed that would not only not disqualify him/her from being hired by your organization, but would actually indicate that he/she might be a particularly good fit?
<--- Score

46. Are data storage and disaster recovery services taxable?
<--- Score

47. Were Pareto charts (or similar) used to portray the 'heavy hitters' (or key sources of variation)?
<--- Score

48. What data is gathered?
<--- Score

49. What qualifications do Digital Content Management leaders need?
<--- Score

50. How has the Digital Content Management data been gathered?
<--- Score

51. What are the best opportunities for value improvement?
<--- Score

52. Is the performance gap determined?
<--- Score

53. How does the organization define, manage, and improve its Digital Content Management processes?
<--- Score

54. Think about some of the processes you undertake within your organization, which do you own?
<--- Score

55. What does the data say about the performance of the stakeholder process?
<--- Score

56. Were any designed experiments used to generate additional insight into the data analysis?
<--- Score

57. What qualifications are necessary?
<--- Score

58. How is the Digital Content Management Value

Stream Mapping managed?
<--- Score

59. What tools were used to narrow the list of possible causes?
<--- Score

60. How difficult is it to qualify what Digital Content Management ROI is?
<--- Score

61. How is the way you as the leader think and process information affecting your organizational culture?
<--- Score

62. Do you understand your management processes today?
<--- Score

63. Are all team members qualified for all tasks?
<--- Score

64. Where can you get qualified talent today?
<--- Score

65. Was a detailed process map created to amplify critical steps of the 'as is' stakeholder process?
<--- Score

66. What tools were used to generate the list of possible causes?
<--- Score

67. What qualifies as competition?
<--- Score

68. How can risk management be tied procedurally to process elements?
<--- Score

69. Who qualifies to gain access to data?
<--- Score

70. Do quality systems drive continuous improvement?
<--- Score

71. What metadata-related acronyms should you be aware of?
<--- Score

72. How are outputs preserved and protected?
<--- Score

73. How is data used for program management and improvement?
<--- Score

74. Record-keeping requirements flow from the records needed as inputs, outputs, controls and for transformation of a Digital Content Management process, are the records needed as inputs to the Digital Content Management process available?
<--- Score

75. A compounding model resolution with available relevant data can often provide insight towards a solution methodology; which Digital Content Management models, tools and techniques are necessary?
<--- Score

76. Identify an operational issue in your organization, for example, could a particular task be done more quickly or more efficiently by Digital Content Management?
<--- Score

77. How much data can be collected in the given timeframe?
<--- Score

78. What, related to, Digital Content Management processes does your organization outsource?
<--- Score

79. Is data and process analysis, root cause analysis and quantifying the gap/opportunity in place?
<--- Score

80. How will the data be checked for quality?
<--- Score

81. What is the output?
<--- Score

82. What resources go in to get the desired output?
<--- Score

83. Is there an established change management process?
<--- Score

84. What qualifications and skills do you need?
<--- Score

85. Are you missing Digital Content Management opportunities?

<--- Score

86. How do you define collaboration and team output?
<--- Score

87. An organizationally feasible system request is one that considers the mission, goals and objectives of the organization, key questions are: is the Digital Content Management solution request practical and will it solve a problem or take advantage of an opportunity to achieve company goals?
<--- Score

88. What is the Value Stream Mapping?
<--- Score

89. What are the personnel training and qualifications required?
<--- Score

90. Is the required Digital Content Management data gathered?
<--- Score

91. What are your current levels and trends in key Digital Content Management measures or indicators of product and process performance that are important to and directly serve your customers?
<--- Score

92. Where do the marketing managers, finance managers and sales managers go to get information about sales opportunities?
<--- Score

93. Are your outputs consistent?
<--- Score

94. What do you need to qualify?
<--- Score

95. What will drive Digital Content Management change?
<--- Score

96. What were the financial benefits resulting from any 'ground fruit or low-hanging fruit' (quick fixes)?
<--- Score

97. What are your best practices for minimizing Digital Content Management project risk, while demonstrating incremental value and quick wins throughout the Digital Content Management project lifecycle?
<--- Score

98. Who is involved with workflow mapping?
<--- Score

99. Can you add value to the current Digital Content Management decision-making process (largely qualitative) by incorporating uncertainty modeling (more quantitative)?
<--- Score

100. What information qualified as important?
<--- Score

101. Have you defined which data is gathered how?
<--- Score

102. Who will gather what data?
<--- Score

103. Is there any way to speed up the process?
<--- Score

104. Where is the data coming from to measure compliance?
<--- Score

105. Which Digital Content Management data should be retained?
<--- Score

106. What Digital Content Management data should be collected?
<--- Score

107. Is the Digital Content Management process severely broken such that a re-design is necessary?
<--- Score

108. Where is Digital Content Management data gathered?
<--- Score

109. What Digital Content Management data will be collected?
<--- Score

110. What other organizational variables, such as reward systems or communication systems, affect the performance of this Digital Content Management process?
<--- Score

111. What is the cost of poor quality as supported by the team's analysis?

<--- Score

112. Is digital transformation a risk or an opportunity for your manufacturing organization?

<--- Score

113. What methods do you use to gather Digital Content Management data?

<--- Score

114. How do your work systems and key work processes relate to and capitalize on your core competencies?

<--- Score

115. What is the Digital Content Management Driver?

<--- Score

116. What process improvements will be needed?

<--- Score

117. What conclusions were drawn from the team's data collection and analysis? How did the team reach these conclusions?

<--- Score

118. Do your employees have the opportunity to do what they do best everyday?

<--- Score

119. Think about the functions involved in your Digital Content Management project, what processes flow from these functions?

<--- Score

120. Are there different types of metadata?
<--- Score

121. Who owns what data?
<--- Score

122. What is the oversight process?
<--- Score

123. What process should you select for improvement?
<--- Score

124. Who gets your output?
<--- Score

125. Do you, as a leader, bounce back quickly from setbacks?
<--- Score

126. Are Digital Content Management changes recognized early enough to be approved through the regular process?
<--- Score

127. What systems/processes must you excel at?
<--- Score

128. What is your organizations system for selecting qualified vendors?
<--- Score

129. When should a process be art not science?
<--- Score

130. What Digital Content Management data should be managed?
<--- Score

131. How do mission and objectives affect the Digital Content Management processes of your organization?
<--- Score

132. Were there any improvement opportunities identified from the process analysis?
<--- Score

133. What are evaluation criteria for the output?
<--- Score

134. Who will facilitate the team and process?
<--- Score

Add up total points for this section:
_____ = Total points for this section

Divided by: _____ (number of statements answered) = _____
Average score for this section

Transfer your score to the Digital Content Management Index at the beginning of the Self-Assessment.

CRITERION #5: IMPROVE:

INTENT: Develop a practical solution. Innovate, establish and test the solution and to measure the results.

In my belief, the answer to this question is clearly defined:

5 Strongly Agree

4 Agree

3 Neutral

2 Disagree

1 Strongly Disagree

1. What are the concrete Digital Content Management results?
<--- Score

2. How will you recognize and celebrate results?
<--- Score

3. What are the Digital Content Management security risks?

<--- Score

4. What tools were used to evaluate the potential solutions?
<--- Score

5. How significant is the improvement in the eyes of the end user?
<--- Score

6. Are the key business and technology risks being managed?
<--- Score

7. Is Digital Content Management documentation maintained?
<--- Score

8. What improvements have been achieved?
<--- Score

9. Do those selected for the Digital Content Management team have a good general understanding of what Digital Content Management is all about?
<--- Score

10. What resources are required for the improvement efforts?
<--- Score

11. Are events managed to resolution?
<--- Score

12. How do you keep improving Digital Content Management?

<--- Score

13. What are the implications of the one critical Digital Content Management decision 10 minutes, 10 months, and 10 years from now?
<--- Score

14. What types of electronic documents?
<--- Score

15. What should a proof of concept or pilot accomplish?
<--- Score

16. How is knowledge sharing about risk management improved?
<--- Score

17. Is the Digital Content Management documentation thorough?
<--- Score

18. What error proofing will be done to address some of the discrepancies observed in the 'as is' process?
<--- Score

19. How will you know that a change is an improvement?
<--- Score

20. Explorations of the frontiers of Digital Content Management will help you build influence, improve Digital Content Management, optimize decision making, and sustain change, what is your approach?
<--- Score

21. Who controls the risk?
<--- Score

22. How do you improve your likelihood of success ?
<--- Score

23. What lessons, if any, from a pilot were incorporated into the design of the full-scale solution?
<--- Score

24. Does your solution support public-facing E-forms that can be filled out and submitted on line?
<--- Score

25. How do you improve Digital Content Management service perception, and satisfaction?
<--- Score

26. What assumptions are made about the solution and approach?
<--- Score

27. What is the team's contingency plan for potential problems occurring in implementation?
<--- Score

28. How do the Digital Content Management results compare with the performance of your competitors and other organizations with similar offerings?
<--- Score

29. What alternative responses are available to manage risk?
<--- Score

30. How can the phases of Digital Content Management development be identified?
<--- Score

31. What strategies for Digital Content Management improvement are successful?
<--- Score

32. Is the Digital Content Management solution sustainable?
<--- Score

33. What is Digital Content Management risk?
<--- Score

34. Who will be responsible for documenting the Digital Content Management requirements in detail?
<--- Score

35. What needs improvement? Why?
<--- Score

36. What is the Digital Content Management's sustainability risk?
<--- Score

37. Who will be using the results of the measurement activities?
<--- Score

38. Which of the recognised risks out of all risks can be most likely transferred?
<--- Score

39. Who are the Digital Content Management decision-makers?

<--- Score

40. What were the criteria for evaluating a Digital Content Management pilot?
<--- Score

41. Who do you report Digital Content Management results to?
<--- Score

42. How do you identify and understand markets?
<--- Score

43. What practices helps your organization to develop its capacity to recognize patterns?
<--- Score

44. Is supporting Digital Content Management documentation required?
<--- Score

45. How do you manage Digital Content Management risk?
<--- Score

46. Is the solution technically practical?
<--- Score

47. What actually has to improve and by how much?
<--- Score

48. What area needs the greatest improvement?
<--- Score

49. Does a good decision guarantee a good outcome?
<--- Score

50. Are decisions made in a timely manner?
<--- Score

51. What risks do you need to manage?
<--- Score

52. Will the controls trigger any other risks?
<--- Score

53. How do you link measurement and risk?
<--- Score

54. Can the solution be designed and implemented within an acceptable time period?
<--- Score

55. Are there electronic documents that also need to be converted?
<--- Score

56. How are Digital Content Management risks managed?
<--- Score

57. How risky is your organization?
<--- Score

58. What were the underlying assumptions on the cost-benefit analysis?
<--- Score

59. How is the pricing decision made?
<--- Score

60. Can you integrate quality management and risk

management?
<--- Score

61. Who should make the Digital Content Management decisions?
<--- Score

62. Does the goal represent a desired result that can be measured?
<--- Score

63. How can you better manage risk?
<--- Score

64. Who are the people involved in developing and implementing Digital Content Management?
<--- Score

65. What went well, what should change, what can improve?
<--- Score

66. What are the affordable Digital Content Management risks?
<--- Score

67. Who manages Digital Content Management risk?
<--- Score

68. Who will be responsible for making the decisions to include or exclude requested changes once Digital Content Management is underway?
<--- Score

69. What Digital Content Management improvements can be made?

<--- Score

70. Do vendor agreements bring new compliance risk
?
<--- Score

71. Are procedures documented for managing Digital
Content Management risks?
<--- Score

72. Who manages supplier risk management in your
organization?
<--- Score

73. How can skill-level changes improve Digital
Content Management?
<--- Score

74. Are the risks fully understood, reasonable and
manageable?
<--- Score

75. In the past few months, what is the smallest
change you have made that has had the biggest
positive result? What was it about that small change
that produced the large return?
<--- Score

76. How do you improve productivity?
<--- Score

77. Do you cover the five essential competencies:
Communication, Collaboration,Innovation,
Adaptability, and Leadership that improve an
organizations ability to leverage the new Digital
Content Management in a volatile global economy?

<--- Score

78. Do you need to do a usability evaluation?
<--- Score

79. Does pricing need to address all software and hardware required to implement the staging a development environments?
<--- Score

80. Have you achieved Digital Content Management improvements?
<--- Score

81. What tools do you use once you have decided on a Digital Content Management strategy and more importantly how do you choose?
<--- Score

82. At what point will vulnerability assessments be performed once Digital Content Management is put into production (e.g., ongoing Risk Management after implementation)?
<--- Score

83. Is any Digital Content Management documentation required?
<--- Score

84. Is there any other Digital Content Management solution?
<--- Score

85. If you could go back in time five years, what decision would you make differently? What is your best guess as to what decision you're making today

you might regret five years from now?

<--- Score

86. How do you measure improved Digital Content Management service perception, and satisfaction?

<--- Score

87. Risk factors: what are the characteristics of Digital Content Management that make it risky?

<--- Score

88. How can you improve Digital Content Management?

<--- Score

89. Does your solution provide access to documents on a public facing online system?

<--- Score

90. How do you manage documents with a retention policy?

<--- Score

91. Is risk periodically assessed?

<--- Score

92. Do you have the optimal project management team structure?

<--- Score

93. What is the implementation plan?

<--- Score

94. Are you assessing Digital Content Management and risk?

<--- Score

95. Are the most efficient solutions problem-specific?
<--- Score

96. How will you know when its improved?
<--- Score

97. Risk Identification: What are the possible risk events your organization faces in relation to Digital Content Management?
<--- Score

98. Why improve in the first place?
<--- Score

99. For estimation problems, how do you develop an estimation statement?
<--- Score

100. Is there a high likelihood that any recommendations will achieve their intended results?
<--- Score

101. Digital Content Management risk decisions: whose call Is It?
<--- Score

102. For decision problems, how do you develop a decision statement?
<--- Score

103. Who are the Digital Content Management decision makers?
<--- Score

104. Are risk management tasks balanced centrally

and locally?
<--- Score

105. How do you define the solutions' scope?
<--- Score

106. Where do the Digital Content Management decisions reside?
<--- Score

107. Does the system have enough document and training materials?
<--- Score

108. Is the scope clearly documented?
<--- Score

109. How do you manage and improve your Digital Content Management work systems to deliver customer value and achieve organizational success and sustainability?
<--- Score

110. How do you deal with Digital Content Management risk?
<--- Score

111. What can you do to improve?
<--- Score

112. Have you identified breakpoints and/or risk tolerances that will trigger broad consideration of a potential need for intervention or modification of strategy?
<--- Score

113. What current systems have to be understood and/or changed?
<--- Score

114. What to do with the results or outcomes of measurements?
<--- Score

115. How is continuous improvement applied to risk management?
<--- Score

116. Is the Digital Content Management risk managed?
<--- Score

117. Was a Digital Content Management charter developed?
<--- Score

118. How do you decide how much to remunerate an employee?
<--- Score

119. What tools were most useful during the improve phase?
<--- Score

120. How will you measure the results?
<--- Score

121. Who are the key stakeholders for the Digital Content Management evaluation?
<--- Score

122. What is the magnitude of the improvements?

<--- Score

123. Risk events: what are the things that could go wrong?
<--- Score

124. How are policy decisions made and where?
<--- Score

125. Where do you need Digital Content Management improvement?
<--- Score

126. Which Digital Content Management solution is appropriate?
<--- Score

127. Do you combine technical expertise with business knowledge and Digital Content Management Key topics include lifecycles, development approaches, requirements and how to make a business case?
<--- Score

128. How do you mitigate Digital Content Management risk?
<--- Score

129. Would you develop a Digital Content Management Communication Strategy?
<--- Score

130. How do you measure risk?
<--- Score

131. What are the expected Digital Content

Management results?

<--- Score

132. What is Digital Content Management's impact on utilizing the best solution(s)?

<--- Score

133. How do you go about comparing Digital Content Management approaches/solutions?

<--- Score

134. What tools were used to tap into the creativity and encourage 'outside the box' thinking?

<--- Score

135. How scalable is your Digital Content Management solution?

<--- Score

Add up total points for this section:
_ _ _ _ _ = Total points for this section

Divided by: _ _ _ _ _ _ (number of statements answered) = _ _ _ _ _ _ Average score for this section

Transfer your score to the Digital Content Management Index at the beginning of the Self-Assessment.

CRITERION #6: CONTROL:

INTENT: Implement the practical solution. Maintain the performance and correct possible complications.

In my belief, the answer to this question is clearly defined:

5 Strongly Agree

4 Agree

3 Neutral

2 Disagree

1 Strongly Disagree

1. Will the team be available to assist members in planning investigations?
<--- Score

2. Have new or revised work instructions resulted?
<--- Score

3. How do you plan for the cost of succession?
<--- Score

4. Act/Adjust: What Do you Need to Do Differently?
<--- Score

5. Is a response plan established and deployed?
<--- Score

6. Does the Digital Content Management performance meet the customer's requirements?
<--- Score

7. What is the control/monitoring plan?
<--- Score

8. Who will be in control?
<--- Score

9. How do controls support value?
<--- Score

10. What are the critical parameters to watch?
<--- Score

11. Do the viable solutions scale to future needs?
<--- Score

12. How will the process owner verify improvement in present and future sigma levels, process capabilities?
<--- Score

13. What other systems, operations, processes, and infrastructures (hiring practices, staffing, training, incentives/rewards, metrics/dashboards/scorecards, etc.) need updates, additions, changes, or deletions in order to facilitate knowledge transfer and improvements?

<--- Score

14. Can support from partners be adjusted?
<--- Score

15. Who is the Digital Content Management process owner?
<--- Score

16. Are new process steps, standards, and documentation ingrained into normal operations?
<--- Score

17. Who has control over resources?
<--- Score

18. Is there a Digital Content Management Communication plan covering who needs to get what information when?
<--- Score

19. Are pertinent alerts monitored, analyzed and distributed to appropriate personnel?
<--- Score

20. Implementation Planning: is a pilot needed to test the changes before a full roll out occurs?
<--- Score

21. Has the Digital Content Management value of standards been quantified?
<--- Score

22. How widespread is its use?
<--- Score

23. Is there an action plan in case of emergencies?
<--- Score

24. Is new knowledge gained imbedded in the response plan?
<--- Score

25. What other areas of the group might benefit from the Digital Content Management team's improvements, knowledge, and learning?
<--- Score

26. What is your plan to assess your security risks?
<--- Score

27. What key inputs and outputs are being measured on an ongoing basis?
<--- Score

28. What is the recommended frequency of auditing?
<--- Score

29. Who sets the Digital Content Management standards?
<--- Score

30. Is the Digital Content Management test/ monitoring cost justified?
<--- Score

31. What is your theory of human motivation, and how does your compensation plan fit with that view?
<--- Score

32. How will new or emerging customer needs/ requirements be checked/communicated to orient

the process toward meeting the new specifications and continually reducing variation?
<--- Score

33. How will input, process, and output variables be checked to detect for sub-optimal conditions?
<--- Score

34. How likely is the current Digital Content Management plan to come in on schedule or on budget?
<--- Score

35. How will the process owner and team be able to hold the gains?
<--- Score

36. Will your goals reflect your program budget?
<--- Score

37. Does job training on the documented procedures need to be part of the process team's education and training?
<--- Score

38. How will report readings be checked to effectively monitor performance?
<--- Score

39. Are operating procedures consistent?
<--- Score

40. Will any special training be provided for results interpretation?
<--- Score

41. Are the planned controls working?
<--- Score

42. Is a response plan in place for when the input, process, or output measures indicate an 'out-of-control' condition?
<--- Score

43. Are there documented procedures?
<--- Score

44. Has the improved process and its steps been standardized?
<--- Score

45. How do you spread information?
<--- Score

46. How might the group capture best practices and lessons learned so as to leverage improvements?
<--- Score

47. When and how frequently do you review you data management plan?
<--- Score

48. What should the next improvement project be that is related to Digital Content Management?
<--- Score

49. What are you attempting to measure/monitor?
<--- Score

50. Is there a transfer of ownership and knowledge to process owner and process team tasked with the responsibilities.

<--- Score

51. Does a troubleshooting guide exist or is it needed?
<--- Score

52. Can you adapt and adjust to changing Digital Content Management situations?
<--- Score

53. How do you select, collect, align, and integrate Digital Content Management data and information for tracking daily operations and overall organizational performance, including progress relative to strategic objectives and action plans?
<--- Score

54. Are controls in place and consistently applied?
<--- Score

55. What do your reports reflect?
<--- Score

56. Do you monitor the Digital Content Management decisions made and fine tune them as they evolve?
<--- Score

57. Is there documentation that will support the successful operation of the improvement?
<--- Score

58. How do you follow and use standards?
<--- Score

59. How will the day-to-day responsibilities for monitoring and continual improvement be transferred from the improvement team to the

process owner?
<--- Score

60. Do you monitor the effectiveness of your Digital Content Management activities?
<--- Score

61. Is reporting being used or needed?
<--- Score

62. What quality tools were useful in the control phase?
<--- Score

63. What are the known security controls?
<--- Score

64. Is there a recommended audit plan for routine surveillance inspections of Digital Content Management's gains?
<--- Score

65. What is the best design framework for Digital Content Management organization now that, in a post industrial-age if the top-down, command and control model is no longer relevant?
<--- Score

66. Is there a control plan in place for sustaining improvements (short and long-term)?
<--- Score

67. Are documented procedures clear and easy to follow for the operators?
<--- Score

68. Where do ideas that reach policy makers and planners as proposals for Digital Content Management strengthening and reform actually originate?
<--- Score

69. Is knowledge gained on process shared and institutionalized?
<--- Score

70. How do you monitor usage and cost?
<--- Score

71. How do senior leaders actions reflect a commitment to the organizations Digital Content Management values?
<--- Score

72. Does Digital Content Management appropriately measure and monitor risk?
<--- Score

73. What Digital Content Management standards are applicable?
<--- Score

74. How do you establish and deploy modified action plans if circumstances require a shift in plans and rapid execution of new plans?
<--- Score

75. Is there a documented and implemented monitoring plan?
<--- Score

76. Are suggested corrective/restorative actions

indicated on the response plan for known causes to problems that might surface?
<--- Score

77. Does the response plan contain a definite closed loop continual improvement scheme (e.g., plan-do-check-act)?
<--- Score

78. Is there a standardized process?
<--- Score

79. How do your controls stack up?
<--- Score

80. Do the Digital Content Management decisions you make today help people and the planet tomorrow?
<--- Score

81. In the case of a Digital Content Management project, the criteria for the audit derive from implementation objectives, an audit of a Digital Content Management project involves assessing whether the recommendations outlined for implementation have been met, can you track that any Digital Content Management project is implemented as planned, and is it working?
<--- Score

82. What adjustments to the strategies are needed?
<--- Score

83. What are the Research and Development (R&D), and standardization priorities?
<--- Score

84. Are the planned controls in place?
<--- Score

85. Are the Digital Content Management standards challenging?
<--- Score

86. How do you encourage people to take control and responsibility?
<--- Score

87. How do you plan on providing proper recognition and disclosure of supporting companies?
<--- Score

88. How is Digital Content Management project cost planned, managed, monitored?
<--- Score

89. What are your results for key measures or indicators of the accomplishment of your Digital Content Management strategy and action plans, including building and strengthening core competencies?
<--- Score

90. What are the performance and scale of the Digital Content Management tools?
<--- Score

91. Who is going to spread your message?
<--- Score

92. Does security from the legacy system need to be mapped into the plan?
<--- Score

Add up total points for this section:
_ _ _ _ _ = Total points for this section

Divided by: _ _ _ _ _ _ (number of
statements answered) = _ _ _ _ _ _
Average score for this section

Transfer your score to the Digital
Content Management Index at the
beginning of the Self-Assessment.

CRITERION #7: SUSTAIN:

INTENT: Retain the benefits.

In my belief, the answer to this question is clearly defined:

5 Strongly Agree

4 Agree

3 Neutral

2 Disagree

1 Strongly Disagree

1. How do you keep the momentum going?
<--- Score

2. Can you do all this work?
<--- Score

3. Is your basic point _____ or _____?
<--- Score

4. What are the rules and assumptions your industry operates under? What if the opposite were true?

<--- Score

5. Who are the key stakeholders?
<--- Score

6. Which individuals, teams or departments will be involved in Digital Content Management?
<--- Score

7. What is it like to work for you?
<--- Score

8. Who do we want your customers to become?
<--- Score

9. What was the last experiment you ran?
<--- Score

10. Do you think Digital Content Management accomplishes the goals you expect it to accomplish?
<--- Score

11. What are the essentials of internal Digital Content Management management?
<--- Score

12. How do you ensure that implementations of Digital Content Management products are done in a way that ensures safety?
<--- Score

13. Are your responses positive or negative?
<--- Score

14. How do you deal with Digital Content Management changes?

<--- Score

15. If your company went out of business tomorrow, would anyone who doesn't get a paycheck here care?
<--- Score

16. What management system can you use to leverage the Digital Content Management experience, ideas, and concerns of the people closest to the work to be done?
<--- Score

17. Are you making progress, and are you making progress as Digital Content Management leaders?
<--- Score

18. Does the ecm fully integrate with Microsoft Office applications (word, excel, powerpoint, etc.)?
<--- Score

19. What does your signature ensure?
<--- Score

20. Do you say no to customers for no reason?
<--- Score

21. What is an unauthorized commitment?
<--- Score

22. How do you transition from the baseline to the target?
<--- Score

23. Who are your customers?
<--- Score

24. How do you cross-sell and up-sell your Digital Content Management success?
<--- Score

25. What are your most important goals for the strategic Digital Content Management objectives?
<--- Score

26. In retrospect, of the projects that you pulled the plug on, what percent do you wish had been allowed to keep going, and what percent do you wish had ended earlier?
<--- Score

27. Who is responsible for errors?
<--- Score

28. What is your question? Why?
<--- Score

29. What are strategies for increasing support and reducing opposition?
<--- Score

30. What is the funding source for this project?
<--- Score

31. What Digital Content Management modifications can you make work for you?
<--- Score

32. What are the barriers to increased Digital Content Management production?
<--- Score

33. How do you proactively clarify deliverables and

Digital Content Management quality expectations?
<--- Score

34. What is the kind of project structure that would
be appropriate for your Digital Content Management
project, should it be formal and complex, or can it be
less formal and relatively simple?
<--- Score

**35. Which technologies does your organization
use to manage content?**
<--- Score

36. Will there be any necessary staff changes
(redundancies or new hires)?
<--- Score

37. Ask yourself: how would you do this work if you
only had one staff member to do it?
<--- Score

38. How do you set Digital Content Management
stretch targets and how do you get people to not only
participate in setting these stretch targets but also
that they strive to achieve these?
<--- Score

39. How do you foster innovation?
<--- Score

40. How do you accomplish your long range Digital
Content Management goals?
<--- Score

41. What is the recommended frequency of auditing?
<--- Score

42. What are the long-term Digital Content Management goals?
<--- Score

43. How much contingency will be available in the budget?
<--- Score

44. Think of your Digital Content Management project, what are the main functions?
<--- Score

45. How do you make it meaningful in connecting Digital Content Management with what users do day-to-day?
<--- Score

46. How can you become more high-tech but still be high touch?
<--- Score

47. What are the goals of preserving your digital content?
<--- Score

48. What are the business goals Digital Content Management is aiming to achieve?
<--- Score

49. What is the overall talent health of your organization as a whole at senior levels, and for each organization reporting to a member of the Senior Leadership Team?
<--- Score

50. Who is managing the content?
<--- Score

51. What have been your experiences in defining long range Digital Content Management goals?
<--- Score

52. Why should people listen to you?
<--- Score

53. If you weren't already in this business, would you enter it today? And if not, what are you going to do about it?
<--- Score

54. Which models, tools and techniques are necessary?
<--- Score

55. Who is on the team?
<--- Score

56. Why is Digital Content Management important for you now?
<--- Score

57. What goals did you miss?
<--- Score

58. What happens when a new employee joins the organization?
<--- Score

59. Is Digital Content Management realistic, or are you setting yourself up for failure?
<--- Score

60. Do you have an implicit bias for capital investments over people investments?
<--- Score

61. Are you satisfied with your current role? If not, what is missing from it?
<--- Score

62. How do you go about securing Digital Content Management?
<--- Score

63. How are you doing compared to your industry?
<--- Score

64. When will you deliver customer satisfaction?
<--- Score

65. What one word do you want to own in the minds of your customers, employees, and partners?
<--- Score

66. What would put your organization on a path to success for content management and production?
<--- Score

67. Are you / should you be revolutionary or evolutionary?
<--- Score

68. Is a Digital Content Management team work effort in place?
<--- Score

69. What happens at your organization when people

fail?

<--- Score

70. Whose voice (department, ethnic group, women, older workers, etc) might you have missed hearing from in your company, and how might you amplify this voice to create positive momentum for your business?

<--- Score

71. Do you feel that more should be done in the Digital Content Management area?

<--- Score

72. Have benefits been optimized with all key stakeholders?

<--- Score

73. Can you maintain your growth without detracting from the factors that have contributed to your success?

<--- Score

74. Will it be accepted by users?

<--- Score

75. Is your strategy driving your strategy? Or is the way in which you allocate resources driving your strategy?

<--- Score

76. What potential megatrends could make your business model obsolete?

<--- Score

77. What unique value proposition (UVP) do you offer?

<--- Score

78. Why are producers who use direct distribution in the minority?
<--- Score

79. What are the potential basics of Digital Content Management fraud?
<--- Score

80. How important is Digital Content Management to the user organizations mission?
<--- Score

81. If your customer were your grandmother, would you tell her to buy what you're selling?
<--- Score

82. What you are going to do to affect the numbers?
<--- Score

83. Is there any existing Digital Content Management governance structure?
<--- Score

84. How do producers get products and services to target customers?
<--- Score

85. What new services of functionality will be implemented next with Digital Content Management ?
<--- Score

86. Is there any reason to believe the opposite of my current belief?

<--- Score

87. What is effective Digital Content Management?
<--- Score

88. How do you stay inspired?
<--- Score

89. How can you incorporate support to ensure safe
and effective use of Digital Content Management into
the services that you provide?
<--- Score

90. What is your Digital Content Management
strategy?
<--- Score

91. Is the impact that Digital Content Management
has shown?
<--- Score

92. Who else should you help?
<--- Score

93. Is it economical; do you have the time and money?
<--- Score

94. What business benefits will Digital Content
Management goals deliver if achieved?
<--- Score

95. How does Digital Content Management integrate
with other stakeholder initiatives?
<--- Score

96. Are you relevant? Will you be relevant five years

from now? Ten?

<--- Score

97. Why think of Enterprise Information Management?

<--- Score

98. What is the source of the strategies for Digital Content Management strengthening and reform?

<--- Score

99. How do you assess the Digital Content Management pitfalls that are inherent in implementing it?

<--- Score

100. How will you motivate the stakeholders with the least vested interest?

<--- Score

101. What are the gaps in your knowledge and experience?

<--- Score

102. Why do and why don't your customers like your organization?

<--- Score

103. How would you describe the scalability of your organizations content-related efforts?

<--- Score

104. How does the sales tax apply?

<--- Score

105. If you got fired and a new hire took your place,

what would she do different?
<--- Score

106. How do you manage Digital Content Management Knowledge Management (KM)?
<--- Score

107. How do you create buy-in?
<--- Score

108. What is the range of capabilities?
<--- Score

109. Instead of going to current contacts for new ideas, what if you reconnected with dormant contacts--the people you used to know? If you were going reactivate a dormant tie, who would it be?
<--- Score

110. Who is responsible for ensuring appropriate resources (time, people and money) are allocated to Digital Content Management?
<--- Score

111. What is your BATNA (best alternative to a negotiated agreement)?
<--- Score

112. What are the products unique features?
<--- Score

113. What may be the consequences for the performance of an organization if all stakeholders are not consulted regarding Digital Content Management?
<--- Score

114. Can you break it down?
<--- Score

115. Did your employees make progress today?
<--- Score

116. What must you excel at?
<--- Score

117. What relationships among Digital Content Management trends do you perceive?
<--- Score

118. What are your personal philosophies regarding Digital Content Management and how do they influence your work?
<--- Score

119. Who are four people whose careers you have enhanced?
<--- Score

120. What counts that you are not counting?
<--- Score

121. How will you deliver customer satisfaction?
<--- Score

122. Would you rather sell to knowledgeable and informed customers or to uninformed customers?
<--- Score

123. What stupid rule would you most like to kill?
<--- Score

124. Have new benefits been realized?
<--- Score

125. How do you govern and fulfill your societal responsibilities?
<--- Score

126. Who, on the executive team or the board, has spoken to a customer recently?
<--- Score

127. How likely is it that a customer would recommend your company to a friend or colleague?
<--- Score

128. What will be the consequences to the stakeholder (financial, reputation etc) if Digital Content Management does not go ahead or fails to deliver the objectives?
<--- Score

129. How do you listen to customers to obtain actionable information?
<--- Score

130. Why should you adopt a Digital Content Management framework?
<--- Score

131. What is the estimated value of the project?
<--- Score

132. How are you measuring content effectiveness?
<--- Score

133. Who have you, as a company, historically been when you've been at your best?
<--- Score

134. Can the schedule be done in the given time?
<--- Score

135. Do you obtain a list of your organizations that indicated intent to submit a response to an RFP?
<--- Score

136. How will this be distributed?
<--- Score

137. Who are your present customers and why do they buy from you?
<--- Score

138. Who uses your product in ways you never expected?
<--- Score

139. How good is the systems search capability?
<--- Score

140. How many employees do you have assigned to your ECM Suite related tasks?
<--- Score

141. How is implementation research currently incorporated into each of your goals?
<--- Score

142. Does your organization have a content marketing strategy?
<--- Score

143. Will you have a single, unified workflow for everyone creating customer-facing content?
<--- Score

144. What are you trying to prove to yourself, and how might it be hijacking your life and business success?
<--- Score

145. Are the criteria for selecting recommendations stated?
<--- Score

146. When is the first return due for a vendor of taxable computer or software services?
<--- Score

147. How can you negotiate Digital Content Management successfully with a stubborn boss, an irate client, or a deceitful coworker?
<--- Score

148. What are you challenging?
<--- Score

149. What do you stand for--and what are you against?
<--- Score

150. Is the Digital Content Management organization completing tasks effectively and efficiently?
<--- Score

151. Are you using a design thinking approach and integrating Innovation, Digital Content Management Experience, and Brand Value?

<--- Score

152. Is this subject to sales tax?
<--- Score

153. What is the craziest thing you can do?
<--- Score

154. Do you think you know, or do you know you know ?
<--- Score

155. Does culture lead or follow structural shifts?
<--- Score

156. What should you stop doing?
<--- Score

157. Is there a work around that you can use?
<--- Score

158. What are the short and long-term Digital Content Management goals?
<--- Score

159. What would have to be true for the option on the table to be the best possible choice?
<--- Score

160. What are internal and external Digital Content Management relations?
<--- Score

161. What happens if you do not have enough funding?
<--- Score

162. Do you see more potential in people than they do in themselves?
<--- Score

163. Do you have past Digital Content Management successes?
<--- Score

164. Is maximizing Digital Content Management protection the same as minimizing Digital Content Management loss?
<--- Score

165. Who will provide the final approval of Digital Content Management deliverables?
<--- Score

166. Are you paying enough attention to the partners your company depends on to succeed?
<--- Score

167. If you do not follow, then how to lead?
<--- Score

168. What are the challenges?
<--- Score

169. When information truly is ubiquitous, when reach and connectivity are completely global, when computing resources are infinite, and when a whole new set of impossibilities are not only possible, but happening, what will that do to your business?
<--- Score

170. Do you have enough freaky customers in your

portfolio pushing you to the limit day in and day out?
<--- Score

171. What is the big Digital Content Management idea?
<--- Score

172. Are you changing as fast as the world around you?
<--- Score

173. What are the usability implications of Digital Content Management actions?
<--- Score

174. What could happen if you do not do it?
<--- Score

175. Who do you think the world wants your organization to be?
<--- Score

176. What are the digital instructional materials?
<--- Score

177. If you had to leave your organization for a year and the only communication you could have with employees/colleagues was a single paragraph, what would you write?
<--- Score

178. How will you ensure you get what you expected?
<--- Score

179. What is your formula for success in Digital Content Management ?

<--- Score

180. Which Digital Content Management goals are the most important?
<--- Score

181. Can drm restrictions be eased?
<--- Score

182. How do you put it all together?
<--- Score

183. Were lessons learned captured and communicated?
<--- Score

184. How is any customization affected by upgrades?
<--- Score

185. Who will deliver customer satisfaction?
<--- Score

186. Do you have the right people on the bus?
<--- Score

187. How do you keep records, of what?
<--- Score

188. What format are the images stored in?
<--- Score

189. If you were responsible for initiating and implementing major changes in your organization, what steps might you take to ensure acceptance of those changes?

<--- Score

190. What are the top 3 things at the forefront of your Digital Content Management agendas for the next 3 years?
<--- Score

191. How do you engage the workforce, in addition to satisfying them?
<--- Score

192. What is the overall business strategy?
<--- Score

193. Do you know what you are doing? And who do you call if you don't?
<--- Score

194. What role does communication play in the success or failure of a Digital Content Management project?
<--- Score

195. Will giving away some free products enhance sales?
<--- Score

196. Are new benefits received and understood?
<--- Score

197. What do we do when new problems arise?
<--- Score

198. How do senior leaders deploy your organizations vision and values through your leadership system, to the workforce, to key suppliers and partners, and to

customers and other stakeholders, as appropriate?
<--- Score

199. Is a Digital Content Management breakthrough on the horizon?
<--- Score

200. Where will you deliver customer satisfaction?
<--- Score

201. Who is responsible for Digital Content Management?
<--- Score

202. If no one would ever find out about your accomplishments, how would you lead differently?
<--- Score

203. Who will manage the integration of tools?
<--- Score

204. How do you approach marketing to different areas of the world?
<--- Score

205. Do you know who is a friend or a foe?
<--- Score

206. How do customers see your organization?
<--- Score

207. What information is critical to your organization that your executives are ignoring?
<--- Score

208. What did you miss in the interview for the worst

hire you ever made?
<--- Score

209. How do you lead with Digital Content Management in mind?
<--- Score

210. What trophy do you want on your mantle?
<--- Score

211. Who will benefit from this program?
<--- Score

212. Did you create a preservation policy?
<--- Score

213. Marketing budgets are tighter, consumers are more skeptical, and social media has changed forever the way we talk about Digital Content Management, how do you gain traction?
<--- Score

214. Which functions and people interact with the supplier and or customer?
<--- Score

215. Are the assumptions believable and achievable?
<--- Score

216. What is your competitive advantage?
<--- Score

217. How will you gain advantage over competitors?
<--- Score

218. Who do you want your customers to become?
<--- Score

219. How do you provide a safe environment
-physically and emotionally?
<--- Score

220. Is this a service or a product?
<--- Score

221. How does your organization demonstrate good practice?
<--- Score

222. Do you have the right capabilities and capacities?
<--- Score

223. Political -is anyone trying to undermine this project?
<--- Score

224. How will commissions be handled?
<--- Score

225. Are assumptions made in Digital Content Management stated explicitly?
<--- Score

226. How will you insure seamless interoperability of Digital Content Management moving forward?
<--- Score

227. How do you determine the key elements that affect Digital Content Management workforce satisfaction, how are these elements determined for different workforce groups and segments?

<--- Score

228. What Digital Content Management skills are most important?
<--- Score

229. What is something you believe that nearly no one agrees with you on?
<--- Score

230. How much storage capacity is there?
<--- Score

231. How are the units created by the grouping structure linked and coordinated?
<--- Score

232. In the past year, what have you done (or could you have done) to increase the accurate perception of your company/brand as ethical and honest?
<--- Score

233. What changes in your workflow have you found to be the most helpful or important?
<--- Score

234. Who will be responsible for deciding whether Digital Content Management goes ahead or not after the initial investigations?
<--- Score

235. What would you recommend your friend do if he/she were facing this dilemma?
<--- Score

236. In a project to restructure Digital Content

Management outcomes, which stakeholders would you involve?
<--- Score

237. If there were zero limitations, what would you do differently?
<--- Score

238. What are the success criteria that will indicate that Digital Content Management objectives have been met and the benefits delivered?
<--- Score

239. Who will determine interim and final deadlines?
<--- Score

Add up total points for this section:
_ _ _ _ _ = Total points for this section

Divided by: _ _ _ _ _ _ (number of statements answered) = _ _ _ _ _ _
Average score for this section

Transfer your score to the Digital Content Management Index at the beginning of the Self-Assessment.

Digital Content Management and Managing Projects, Criteria for Project Managers:

1.0 Initiating Process Group: Digital Content Management

1. What do they need to know about the Digital Content Management project?

2. Does the Digital Content Management project team have enough people to execute the Digital Content Management project plan?

3. Who does what?

4. Do you know all the stakeholders impacted by the Digital Content Management project and what needs are?

5. Were resources available as planned?

6. What is the stake of others in your Digital Content Management project?

7. The Digital Content Management project managers have maximum authority in which type of organization?

8. Are there resources to maintain and support the outcome of the Digital Content Management project?

9. How can you make your needs known?

10. Based on your Digital Content Management project communication management plan, what worked well?

11. Were decisions made in a timely manner?

12. How well did the chosen processes produce the expected results?

13. How will it affect me?

14. How will you do it?

15. During which stage of Risk planning are modeling techniques used to determine overall effects of risks on Digital Content Management project objectives for high probability, high impact risks?

16. What are the constraints?

17. What will you do to minimize the impact should a risk event occur?

18. Did the Digital Content Management project team have the right skills?

19. Measurable - are the targets measurable?

20. For technology Digital Content Management projects only: Are all production support stakeholders (Business unit, technical support, & user) prepared for implementation with appropriate contingency plans?

1.1 Project Charter: Digital Content Management

21. What barriers do you predict to your success?

22. How are Digital Content Management projects different from operations?

23. Customer benefits: what customer requirements does this Digital Content Management project address?

24. What outcome, in measureable terms, are you hoping to accomplish?

25. Does the Digital Content Management project need to consider any special capacity or capability issues?

26. When will this occur?

27. What material?

28. Pop quiz – which are the same inputs as in the Digital Content Management project charter?

29. Digital Content Management project objective statement: what must the Digital Content Management project do?

30. Why the improvements?

31. Why do you manage integration?

32. When do you use a Digital Content Management project Charter?

33. Digital Content Management project deliverables: what is the Digital Content Management project going to produce?

34. Why is it important?

35. Who is the sponsor?

36. Run it as as a startup?

37. What are you trying to accomplish?

38. Dependent Digital Content Management projects: what Digital Content Management projects must be underway or completed before this Digital Content Management project can be successful?

39. Avoid costs, improve service, and/ or comply with a mandate?

40. What are some examples of a business case?

1.2 Stakeholder Register: Digital Content Management

41. How should employers make voices heard?

42. What are the major Digital Content Management project milestones requiring communications or providing communications opportunities?

43. How big is the gap?

44. Who wants to talk about Security?

45. Is your organization ready for change?

46. Who is managing stakeholder engagement?

47. How much influence do they have on the Digital Content Management project?

48. What & Why?

49. How will reports be created?

50. What opportunities exist to provide communications?

51. Who are the stakeholders?

52. What is the power of the stakeholder?

1.3 Stakeholder Analysis Matrix: Digital Content Management

53. What is your Advocacy Strategy?

54. Organizational Applicability?

55. Effects on core activities, distraction?

56. What do you need to appraise?

57. Experience, knowledge, data?

58. New markets, vertical, horizontal?

59. What is your Risk Management?

60. What is the range you need to look at?

61. Cultural, attitudinal, behavioural?

62. What is accountability in relation to the Digital Content Management project?

63. Competitive advantages?

64. Why do you care?

65. Morale, commitment, leadership?

66. Who has control over whom?

67. Resources, assets, people?

68. What are the mechanisms of public and social accountability, and how can they be made better?

69. Guiding question: what is the issue at stake?

70. Who is most interested in information about the topic and/or has previously initiated interest?

71. What is your organizations competitors doing?

72. Technology development and innovation?

2.0 Planning Process Group: Digital Content Management

73. Did the program design/ implementation strategy adequately address the planning stage necessary to set up structures, hire staff etc.?

74. What factors are contributing to progress or delay in the achievement of products and results?

75. What is the critical path for this Digital Content Management project, and what is the duration of the critical path?

76. How does activity resource estimation affect activity duration estimation?

77. Is the Digital Content Management project supported by national and/or local organizations?

78. What should you do next?

79. In which Digital Content Management project management process group is the detailed Digital Content Management project budget created?

80. Are you just doing busywork to pass the time?

81. In what way has the program contributed towards the issue culture and development included on the public agenda?

82. Have more efficient (sensitive) and appropriate

measures been adopted to respond to the political and socio-cultural problems identified?

83. Is the schedule for the set products being met?

84. Professionals want to know what is expected from them; what are the deliverables?

85. Are work methodologies, financial instruments, etc. shared among departments, organizations and Digital Content Management projects?

86. What business situation is being addressed?

87. In what ways can the governance of the Digital Content Management project be improved so that it has greater likelihood of achieving future sustainability?

88. How are the principles of aid effectiveness (ownership, alignment, management for development results and mutual responsibility) being applied in the Digital Content Management project?

89. How should needs be met?

90. How many days can task X be late in starting without affecting the Digital Content Management project completion date?

91. Explanation: is what the Digital Content Management project intents to solve a hard question?

2.1 Project Management Plan: Digital Content Management

92. Will you add a schedule and diagram?

93. Did the planning effort collaborate to develop solutions that integrate expertise, policies, programs, and Digital Content Management projects across entities?

94. Is there anything you would now do differently on your Digital Content Management project based on past experience?

95. Does the implementation plan have an appropriate division of responsibilities?

96. What went right?

97. Do the proposed changes from the Digital Content Management project include any significant risks to safety?

98. Are calculations and results of analyzes essentially correct?

99. What worked well?

100. If the Digital Content Management project management plan is a comprehensive document that guides you in Digital Content Management project execution and control, then what should it NOT contain?

101. What is the business need?

102. Are there any windfall benefits that would accrue to the Digital Content Management project sponsor or other parties?

103. What are the assumptions?

104. What is Digital Content Management project scope management?

105. What happened during the process that you found interesting?

106. How do you manage time?

107. What if, for example, the positive direction and vision of your organization causes expected trends to change resulting in greater need than expected?

108. Is mitigation authorized or recommended?

2.2 Scope Management Plan: Digital Content Management

109. Organizational unit (e.g., department, team, or person) who will accept responsibility for satisfactory completion of the item?

110. Are you doing what you have set out to do?

111. Were Digital Content Management project team members involved in detailed estimating and scheduling?

112. Why is a scope management plan important?

113. Function of the configuration control board?

114. Are staff skills known and available for each task?

115. Timeline and milestones?

116. Have adequate resources been provided by management to ensure Digital Content Management project success?

117. Describe the process for accepting the Digital Content Management project deliverables. Will the Digital Content Management project deliverables become accepted in writing?

118. What does the critical path really mean?

119. Have the procedures for identifying budget

variances been followed?

120. Are cause and effect determined for risks when they occur?

121. What threats might prevent you from getting there?

122. Has the business need been clearly defined?

123. Have all involved Digital Content Management project stakeholders and work groups committed to the Digital Content Management project?

124. Is pert / critical path or equivalent methodology being used?

125. Does the detailed work plan match the complexity of tasks with the capabilities of personnel?

126. The greatest degree of uncertainty is encountered during which phase of the Digital Content Management project life cycle?

127. Is it possible to track all classes of Digital Content Management project work (e.g. scheduled, un-scheduled, defect repair, etc.)?

2.3 Requirements Management Plan: Digital Content Management

128. Will the product release be stable and mature enough to be deployed in the user community?

129. Who has the authority to reject Digital Content Management project requirements?

130. Who will initially review the Digital Content Management project work or products to ensure it meets the applicable acceptance criteria?

131. Who is responsible for quantifying the Digital Content Management project requirements?

132. Will you use tracing to help understand the impact of a change in requirements?

133. What information regarding the Digital Content Management project requirements will be reported?

134. To see if a requirement statement is sufficiently well-defined, read it from the developers perspective. Mentally add the phrase, call me when youre done to the end of the requirement and see if that makes you nervous. In other words, would you need additional clarification from the author to understand the requirement well enough to design and implement it?

135. Who will perform the analysis?

136. Which hardware or software, related to, or as

outcome of the Digital Content Management project is new to your organization?

137. Is there formal agreement on who has authority to request a change in requirements?

138. Did you provide clear and concise specifications?

139. Do you know which stakeholders will participate in the requirements effort?

140. Did you distinguish the scope of work the contractor(s) will be required to do?

141. In case of software development; Should you have a test for each code module?

142. Is any organizational data being used or stored?

143. Who will approve the requirements (and if multiple approvers, in what order)?

144. How will bidders price evaluations be done, by deliverables, phases, or in a big bang?

145. Will you perform a Requirements Risk assessment and develop a plan to deal with risks?

146. Is infrastructure setup part of your Digital Content Management project?

147. Who will do the reporting and to whom will reports be delivered?

2.4 Requirements Documentation: Digital Content Management

148. What is the risk associated with cost and schedule?

149. What is a show stopper in the requirements?

150. Where do system and software requirements come from, what are sources?

151. How to document system requirements?

152. Is the requirement properly understood?

153. Do your constraints stand?

154. If applicable; are there issues linked with the fact that this is an offshore Digital Content Management project?

155. Consistency. are there any requirements conflicts?

156. How does what is being described meet the business need?

157. Can you check system requirements?

158. What can tools do for us?

159. What if the system wasn t implemented?

160. What are the acceptance criteria?

161. Can the requirement be changed without a large impact on other requirements?

162. What variations exist for a process?

163. Are all functions required by the customer included?

164. Are there legal issues?

165. How will the proposed Digital Content Management project help?

166. What will be the integration problems?

167. Who is interacting with the system?

2.5 Requirements Traceability Matrix: Digital Content Management

168. How do you manage scope?

169. Describe the process for approving requirements so they can be added to the traceability matrix and Digital Content Management project work can be performed. Will the Digital Content Management project requirements become approved in writing?

170. Why do you manage scope?

171. What percentage of Digital Content Management projects are producing traceability matrices between requirements and other work products?

172. What is the WBS?

173. Will you use a Requirements Traceability Matrix?

174. How will it affect the stakeholders personally in career?

175. What are the chronologies, contingencies, consequences, criteria?

176. How small is small enough?

177. Is there a requirements traceability process in place?

178. Do you have a clear understanding of all

subcontracts in place?

179. Why use a WBS?

2.6 Project Scope Statement: Digital Content Management

180. If there are vendors, have they signed off on the Digital Content Management project Plan?

181. Is the plan for Digital Content Management project resources adequate?

182. Is this process communicated to the customer and team members?

183. Is the Digital Content Management project organization documented and on file?

184. Relevant - ask yourself can you get there; why are you doing this Digital Content Management project?

185. Will the risk documents be filed?

186. Change management vs. change leadership - what is the difference?

187. Is the Digital Content Management project sponsor function identified and defined?

188. How will you verify the accuracy of the work of the Digital Content Management project, and what constitutes acceptance of the deliverables?

189. Have you been able to easily identify success criteria and create objective measurements for each of the Digital Content Management project scopes

goal statements?

190. What is change?

191. Will this process be communicated to the customer and Digital Content Management project team?

192. Will tasks be marked complete only after QA has been successfully completed?

193. Who will you recommend approve the change, and when do you recommend the change reviews occur?

194. Is there a process (test plans, inspections, reviews) defined for verifying outputs for each task?

195. Elements of scope management that deal with concept development ?

196. Has a method and process for requirement tracking been developed?

197. How often will scope changes be reviewed?

198. Will all Digital Content Management project issues be unconditionally tracked through the issue resolution process?

199. Do you anticipate new stakeholders joining the Digital Content Management project over time?

2.7 Assumption and Constraint Log: Digital Content Management

200. Does a documented Digital Content Management project organizational policy & plan (i.e. governance model) exist?

201. What do you audit?

202. Is the amount of effort justified by the anticipated value of forming a new process?

203. Are best practices and metrics employed to identify issues, progress, performance, etc.?

204. If appropriate, is the deliverable content consistent with current Digital Content Management project documents and in compliance with the Document Management Plan?

205. Are there cosmetic errors that hinder readability and comprehension?

206. Diagrams and tables are included to account for complex concepts and increase overall readability?

207. Is this model reasonable?

208. What other teams / processes would be impacted by changes to the current process, and how?

209. Is staff trained on the software technologies that are being used on the Digital Content Management

project?

210. Was the document/deliverable developed per the appropriate or required standards (for example, Institute of Electrical and Electronics Engineers standards)?

211. Is there documentation of system capability requirements, data requirements, environment requirements, security requirements, and computer and hardware requirements?

212. Have adequate resources been provided by management to ensure Digital Content Management project success?

213. Has the approach and development strategy of the Digital Content Management project been defined, documented and accepted by the appropriate stakeholders?

214. Is this process still needed?

215. How do you design an auditing system?

216. When can log be discarded?

217. What strengths do you have?

218. Have you eliminated all duplicative tasks or manual efforts, where appropriate?

2.8 Work Breakdown Structure: Digital Content Management

219. Is it still viable?

220. Why is it useful?

221. Where does it take place?

222. Why would you develop a Work Breakdown Structure?

223. How many levels?

224. How much detail?

225. Can you make it?

226. How big is a work-package?

227. When do you stop?

228. What has to be done?

229. Is it a change in scope?

230. What is the probability of completing the Digital Content Management project in less that xx days?

231. When does it have to be done?

232. How far down?

233. Who has to do it?

234. Do you need another level?

2.9 WBS Dictionary: Digital Content Management

235. What is the goal?

236. Are data elements (BCWS, BCWP, and ACWP) progressively summarized from the detail level to the contract level through the CWBS?

237. Does the contractors system provide unit costs, equivalent unit or lot costs in terms of labor, material, other direct, and indirect costs?

238. Changes in the direct base to which overhead costs are allocated?

239. Changes in the overhead pool and/or organization structures?

240. Are your organizations and items of cost assigned to each pool identified?

241. Detailed schedules which support control account and work package start and completion dates/events?

242. Are Digital Content Management projected overhead costs in each pool and the associated direct costs used as the basis for establishing interim rates for allocating overhead to contracts?

243. Where learning is used in developing underlying budgets is there a direct relationship between

anticipated learning and time phased budgets?

244. Are budgets or values assigned to work packages and planning packages in terms of dollars, hours, or other measurable units?

245. Contemplated overhead expenditure for each period based on the best information currently available?

246. Is the entire contract planned in time-phased control accounts to the extent practicable?

247. Major functional areas of contract effort?

248. Identify potential or actual budget-based and time-based schedule variances?

249. Are control accounts opened and closed based on the start and completion of work contained therein?

250. Are the procedures for identifying indirect costs to incurring organizations, indirect cost pools, and allocating the costs from the pools to the contracts formally documented?

251. What is wrong with this Digital Content Management project?

252. The wbs is developed as part of a joint planning session. and how do you know that youhave done this right?

253. Authorization to proceed with all authorized work?

254. What size should a work package be?

2.10 Schedule Management Plan: Digital Content Management

255. Is Digital Content Management project status reviewed with the steering and executive teams at appropriate intervals?

256. Were Digital Content Management project team members involved in detailed estimating and scheduling?

257. Are meeting minutes captured and sent out after the meeting?

258. Perform reality checks on schedules – are all tasks included?

259. Is the steering committee active in Digital Content Management project oversight?

260. Has a structured approach been used to break work effort into manageable components (WBS)?

261. Are estimating assumptions and constraints captured?

262. Are the processes for status updates and maintenance defined?

263. Define units of measurement for each resource. For example, are you referencing gallons or liters?

264. Are risk oriented checklists used during risk

identification?

265. Are scheduled deliverables actually delivered?

266. Were Digital Content Management project team members involved in the development of activity & task decomposition?

267. Are the appropriate IT resources adequate to meet planned commitments?

268. Does the schedule have reasonable float?

269. Where is the scheduling tool and who has access to it to view it?

270. Have Digital Content Management project team accountabilities & responsibilities been clearly defined?

271. Is the ims used by all levels of management for Digital Content Management project implementation and control?

272. Is there an issues management plan in place?

273. Have all necessary approvals been obtained?

2.11 Activity List: Digital Content Management

274. In what sequence?

275. What went wrong?

276. How can the Digital Content Management project be displayed graphically to better visualize the activities?

277. What is the LF and LS for each activity?

278. What will be performed?

279. What are you counting on?

280. How do you determine the late start (LS) for each activity?

281. What is the probability the Digital Content Management project can be completed in xx weeks?

282. Where will it be performed?

283. For other activities, how much delay can be tolerated?

284. Is there anything planned that does not need to be here?

285. What went well?

286. How detailed should a Digital Content Management project get?

287. How should ongoing costs be monitored to try to keep the Digital Content Management project within budget?

288. How difficult will it be to do specific activities on this Digital Content Management project?

289. What is your organizations history in doing similar activities?

290. What is the total time required to complete the Digital Content Management project if no delays occur?

291. When do the individual activities need to start and finish?

2.12 Activity Attributes: Digital Content Management

292. Where else does it apply?

293. Why?

294. How many resources do you need to complete the work scope within a limit of X number of days?

295. Resource is assigned to?

296. Can more resources be added?

297. How difficult will it be to do specific activities on this Digital Content Management project?

298. What is missing?

299. Activity: what is Missing?

300. Are the required resources available?

301. How much activity detail is required?

302. Have constraints been applied to the start and finish milestones for the phases?

303. Resources to accomplish the work?

304. Time for overtime?

305. What conclusions/generalizations can you draw

from this?

306. Have you identified the Activity Leveling Priority code value on each activity?

307. Are the required resources available or need to be acquired?

2.13 Milestone List: Digital Content Management

308. Environmental effects?

309. Describe your organizations strengths and core competencies. What factors will make your organization succeed?

310. Timescales, deadlines and pressures?

311. How late can the activity finish?

312. Can you derive how soon can the whole Digital Content Management project finish?

313. Reliability of data, plan predictability?

314. Continuity, supply chain robustness?

315. Vital contracts and partners?

316. Gaps in capabilities?

317. What date will the task finish?

318. How late can the activity start?

319. Identify critical paths (one or more) and which activities are on the critical path?

320. Global influences?

321. Sustaining internal capabilities?

322. When will the Digital Content Management project be complete?

323. Milestone pages should display the UserID of the person who added the milestone. Does a report or query exist that provides this audit information?

324. Describe the industry you are in and the market growth opportunities. What is the market for your technology, product or service?

325. Sustainable financial backing?

326. Political effects?

2.14 Network Diagram: Digital Content Management

327. Will crashing x weeks return more in benefits than it costs?

328. What are the Key Success Factors?

329. Which type of network diagram allows you to depict four types of dependencies?

330. Planning: who, how long, what to do?

331. What job or jobs precede it?

332. Are you on time?

333. What are the Major Administrative Issues?

334. What job or jobs could run concurrently?

335. If the Digital Content Management project network diagram cannot change and you have extra personnel resources, what is the BEST thing to do?

336. Why must you schedule milestones, such as reviews, throughout the Digital Content Management project?

337. Exercise: what is the probability that the Digital Content Management project duration will exceed xx weeks?

338. What is the completion time?

339. What controls the start and finish of a job?

340. What job or jobs follow it?

341. What is the lowest cost to complete this Digital Content Management project in xx weeks?

342. How confident can you be in your milestone dates and the delivery date?

343. Where do schedules come from?

344. Can you calculate the confidence level?

345. What is the probability of completing the Digital Content Management project in less that xx days?

2.15 Activity Resource Requirements: Digital Content Management

346. Do you use tools like decomposition and rolling-wave planning to produce the activity list and other outputs?

347. When does monitoring begin?

348. What are constraints that you might find during the Human Resource Planning process?

349. How many signatures do you require on a check and does this match what is in your policy and procedures?

350. How do you handle petty cash?

351. Why do you do that?

352. Are there unresolved issues that need to be addressed?

353. Which logical relationship does the PDM use most often?

354. What is the Work Plan Standard?

355. Other support in specific areas?

356. Anything else?

2.16 Resource Breakdown Structure: Digital Content Management

357. Is predictive resource analysis being done?

358. The list could probably go on, but, the thing that you would most like to know is, How long & How much?

359. When do they need the information?

360. What is the number one predictor of a groups productivity?

361. Who needs what information?

362. What is the primary purpose of the human resource plan?

363. Who is allowed to perform which functions?

364. How should the information be delivered?

365. Who will be used as a Digital Content Management project team member?

366. How difficult will it be to do specific activities on this Digital Content Management project?

367. Who will use the system?

368. Why time management?

369. What is the difference between % Complete and % work?

370. Why is this important?

371. How can this help you with team building?

372. Which resources should be in the resource pool?

373. What defines a successful Digital Content Management project?

2.17 Activity Duration Estimates: Digital Content Management

374. Consider the history of modern quality management. How have experts such as Deming, Juran, Crosby, and Taguchi affected the quality movement and todays use of Six Sigma?

375. What time management activity should you do NEXT?

376. Are inspections completed to determine if the results comply with the requirements?

377. What are two suggestions for ensuring adequate change control on Digital Content Management projects that involve outside contracts?

378. Does a process exist to determine the probability of risk events?

379. What is the BEST thing for the Digital Content Management project manager to do?

380. Are costs that may be needed to account for Digital Content Management project risks determined?

381. What type of contract was used and why?

382. Are steps identified by which Digital Content Management project documents may be changed?

383. When would a milestone chart be used instead of a bar char?

384. Do scope statements include the Digital Content Management project objectives and expected deliverables?

385. Are changes to the scope managed according to defined procedures?

386. What is the critical path for this Digital Content Management project and how long is it?

387. Do they make sense?

388. How can organizations use a weighted decision matrix to evaluate proposals as part of source selection?

389. Why is activity definition the first process involved in Digital Content Management project time management?

390. Is risk identification completed regularly throughout the Digital Content Management project?

2.18 Duration Estimating Worksheet: Digital Content Management

391. How can the Digital Content Management project be displayed graphically to better visualize the activities?

392. Done before proceeding with this activity or what can be done concurrently?

393. What is your role?

394. Small or large Digital Content Management project?

395. What is the total time required to complete the Digital Content Management project if no delays occur?

396. Why estimate time and cost?

397. What is an Average Digital Content Management project?

398. How should ongoing costs be monitored to try to keep the Digital Content Management project within budget?

399. Do any colleagues have experience with your organization and/or RFPs?

400. What is cost and Digital Content Management project cost management?

401. Is the Digital Content Management project responsive to community need?

402. What are the critical bottleneck activities?

403. What info is needed?

404. Define the work as completely as possible. What work will be included in the Digital Content Management project?

405. What work will be included in the Digital Content Management project?

406. What is next?

407. Value pocket identification & quantification what are value pockets?

408. When, then?

2.19 Project Schedule: Digital Content Management

409. How can slack be negative?

410. Schedule/cost recovery?

411. Why do you need to manage Digital Content Management project Risk?

412. Eliminate unnecessary activities. Are there activities that came from a template or previous Digital Content Management project that are not applicable on this phase of this Digital Content Management project?

413. To what degree is do you feel the entire team was committed to the Digital Content Management project schedule?

414. What is the difference?

415. Did the Digital Content Management project come in under budget?

416. Is there a Schedule Management Plan that establishes the criteria and activities for developing, monitoring and controlling the Digital Content Management project schedule?

417. What does that mean?

418. Are quality inspections and review activities

listed in the Digital Content Management project schedule(s)?

419. Why or why not?

420. Did the Digital Content Management project come in on schedule?

421. Is the Digital Content Management project schedule available for all Digital Content Management project team members to review?

422. Digital Content Management project work estimates Who is managing the work estimate quality of work tasks in the Digital Content Management project schedule?

423. Are procedures defined by which the Digital Content Management project schedule may be changed?

424. How can you address that situation?

425. Are you working on the right risks?

426. Did the final product meet or exceed user expectations?

427. How can you fix it?

2.20 Cost Management Plan: Digital Content Management

428. Is a stakeholder management plan in place that covers topics?

429. What will be the split of responsibilities of progress measurement and controls among the owner, contractor, subcontractors, and vendors?

430. Have process improvement efforts been completed before requirements efforts begin?

431. Are multiple estimation methods being employed?

432. Weve met your goals?

433. Cost / benefit analysis?

434. Is there general agreement & acceptance of the current status and progress of the Digital Content Management project?

435. Are tasks tracked by hours?

436. What weaknesses do you have?

437. Are the results of quality assurance reviews provided to affected groups & individuals?

438. Planning and scheduling responsibilities – How will the responsibilities for planning and scheduling

be allocated?

439. Schedule contingency – how will the schedule contingency be administrated?

440. Digital Content Management project definition & scope?

441. Forecasts – how will the cost to complete the Digital Content Management project be forecast?

442. If you sold 10x widgets on a day, what would the affect on costs be?

443. Are risk triggers captured?

444. Eac -estimate at completion, what is the total job expected to cost?

445. Have lessons learned been conducted after each Digital Content Management project release?

446. Is it possible to track all classes of Digital Content Management project work (e.g. scheduled, un-scheduled, defect repair, etc.)?

447. What are the Digital Content Management project objectives?

2.21 Activity Cost Estimates: Digital Content Management

448. Vac -variance at completion, how much over/ under budget do you expect to be?

449. Can you change your activities?

450. Would you hire them again?

451. What were things that you need to improve?

452. How do you fund change orders?

453. What makes a good expected result statement?

454. Are cost subtotals needed?

455. Maintenance Reserve?

456. How do you treat administrative costs in the activity inventory?

457. How do you change activities?

458. Does the estimator have experience?

459. How many activities should you have?

460. Performance bond should always provide what part of the contract value?

461. What makes a good activity description?

462. Can you delete activities or make them inactive?

463. What happens if you cannot produce the documentation for the single audit?

464. Does the activity serve a common type of customer?

465. What is the activity inventory?

2.22 Cost Estimating Worksheet: Digital Content Management

466. What is the estimated labor cost today based upon this information?

467. Can a trend be established from historical performance data on the selected measure and are the criteria for using trend analysis or forecasting methods met?

468. What can be included?

469. What costs are to be estimated?

470. Identify the timeframe necessary to monitor progress and collect data to determine how the selected measure has changed?

471. What happens to any remaining funds not used?

472. What will others want?

473. Is the Digital Content Management project responsive to community need?

474. Will the Digital Content Management project collaborate with the local community and leverage resources?

475. Is it feasible to establish a control group arrangement?

476. Ask: are others positioned to know, are others credible, and will others cooperate?

477. How will the results be shared and to whom?

478. Who is best positioned to know and assist in identifying corresponding factors?

479. Does the Digital Content Management project provide innovative ways for stakeholders to overcome obstacles or deliver better outcomes?

480. What is the purpose of estimating?

481. What additional Digital Content Management project(s) could be initiated as a result of this Digital Content Management project?

2.23 Cost Baseline: Digital Content Management

482. How likely is it to go wrong?

483. Should a more thorough impact analysis be conducted?

484. Have all approved changes to the schedule baseline been identified and impact on the Digital Content Management project documented?

485. Is there anything you need from upper management in order to be successful?

486. Pcs for your new business. what would the life cycle costs be?

487. Does the suggested change request seem to represent a necessary enhancement to the product?

488. What is the most important thing to do next to make your Digital Content Management project successful?

489. Digital Content Management project goals -should others be reconsidered?

490. Is the cr within Digital Content Management project scope?

491. Is there anything unique in this Digital Content Management projects scope statement that will affect

resources?

492. What do you want to measure ?

493. How concrete were original objectives?

494. Will the Digital Content Management project fail if the change request is not executed?

495. Are there contingencies or conditions related to the acceptance?

496. What is your organizations history in doing similar tasks?

497. Have all approved changes to the cost baseline been identified and impact on the Digital Content Management project documented?

498. Does a process exist for establishing a cost baseline to measure Digital Content Management project performance?

499. Have all the product or service deliverables been accepted by the customer?

2.24 Quality Management Plan: Digital Content Management

500. Is there a procedure for this process?

501. Does a prospective decision remain the same regardless of what the data show is?

502. What are your organizations current levels and trends for the already stated measures related to financial and marketplace performance?

503. How does your organization decide what to measure?

504. Is there a Steering Committee in place?

505. Are there trends or hot spots?

506. Who gets results of work?

507. What process do you use to minimize errors, defects, and rework?

508. How does your organization recruit, hire, and retain new employees?

509. How does your organization make it easy for customers to seek assistance or complain?

510. How does your organization ensure the reliability, accuracy, timeliness, security and accessibility of data and information?

511. What is the Difference Between a QMP and QAPP?

512. How do you field-modify testing procedures?

513. How does your organization determine the requirements and product/service features important to customers?

514. Where do you focus?

515. Are you meeting the quality standards?

516. How are senior leaders, employees, and your organization involved in supporting the community?

517. How long do you retain data?

518. How does your organization manage training and evaluate its effectiveness?

519. Who is approving the QAPP?

2.25 Quality Metrics: Digital Content Management

520. How can the effectiveness of each of the activities be measured?

521. Have risk areas been identified?

522. Is the reporting frequency appropriate?

523. What if the biggest risk to your business were the already stated people who do not complain?

524. What happens if you get an abnormal result?

525. Is there a set of procedures to capture, analyze and act on quality metrics?

526. Why is now the time for quality metrics?

527. How effective are your security tests?

528. What can manufacturing professionals do to ensure quality is seen as an integral part of the entire product lifecycle?

529. What is the benchmark?

530. What metrics do you measure?

531. Are documents on hand to provide explanations of privacy and confidentiality?

532. The metrics–what is being considered?

533. What documentation is required?

534. What is the timeline to meet your goal?

535. Can visual measures help you to filter visualizations of interest?

536. Are quality metrics defined?

537. Were quality attributes reported?

2.26 Process Improvement Plan: Digital Content Management

538. Are you making progress on the improvement framework?

539. Where are you now?

540. Have storage and access mechanisms and procedures been determined?

541. Why quality management?

542. Are you making progress on the goals?

543. Are you following the quality standards?

544. What actions are needed to address the problems and achieve the goals?

545. Modeling current processes is great, and will you ever see a return on that investment?

546. What makes people good SPI coaches?

547. Everyone agrees on what process improvement is, right?

548. Does your process ensure quality?

549. To elicit goal statements, do you ask a question such as, What do you want to achieve?

550. Has the time line required to move measurement results from the points of collection to databases or users been established?

551. What is the return on investment?

552. What personnel are the sponsors for that initiative?

553. What personnel are the change agents for your initiative?

554. What personnel are the coaches for your initiative?

555. What lessons have you learned so far?

556. Management commitment at all levels?

2.27 Responsibility Assignment Matrix: Digital Content Management

557. The staff characteristics – is the group or the person capable to work together as a team?

558. Who is going to do that work?

559. What materials and procurements needed?

560. Are the actual costs used for variance analysis reconcilable with data from the accounting system?

561. Do you know how your people are allocated?

562. Does the contractors system identify work accomplishment against the schedule plan?

563. Does a missing responsibility indicate that the current Digital Content Management project is not yet fully understood?

564. Is work properly classified as measured effort, LOE, or apportioned effort and appropriately separated?

565. Direct labor dollars and/or hours?

566. How many people do you need?

567. Are records maintained to show how management reserves are used?

568. Ideas for developing soft skills at your organization?

569. Does each role with Accountable responsibility have the authority within your organization to make the required decisions?

570. What happens when others get pulled for higher priority Digital Content Management projects?

571. What expertise is available in your department?

572. Are detailed work packages planned as far in advance as practicable?

573. If a role has only Signing-off, or only Communicating responsibility and has no Performing, Accountable, or Monitoring responsibility, is it necessary?

2.28 Roles and Responsibilities: Digital Content Management

574. Was the expectation clearly communicated?

575. Once the responsibilities are defined for the Digital Content Management project, have the deliverables, roles and responsibilities been clearly communicated to every participant?

576. What expectations were NOT met?

577. Where are you most strong as a supervisor?

578. Do the values and practices inherent in the culture of your organization foster or hinder the process?

579. Do you take the time to clearly define roles and responsibilities on Digital Content Management project tasks?

580. What is working well?

581. What should you do now to ensure that you are exceeding expectations and excelling in your current position?

582. What specific behaviors did you observe?

583. What areas of supervision are challenging for you?

584. Is there a training program in place for stakeholders covering expectations, roles and responsibilities and any addition knowledge others need to be good stakeholders?

585. Concern: where are you limited or have no authority, where you can not influence?

586. Have you ever been a part of this team?

587. Are your budgets supportive of a culture of quality data?

588. What should you do now to ensure that you are meeting all expectations of your current position?

589. Are governance roles and responsibilities documented?

590. What should you do now to prepare for your career 5+ years from now?

591. Required skills, knowledge, experience?

592. What is working well within your organizations performance management system?

593. How well did the Digital Content Management project Team understand the expectations of specific roles and responsibilities?

2.29 Human Resource Management Plan: Digital Content Management

594. Is stakeholder involvement adequate?

595. List the assumptions made to date. What did you have to assume to be true to complete the charter?

596. Does a documented Digital Content Management project organizational policy & plan (i.e. governance model) exist?

597. Are vendor contract reports, reviews and visits conducted periodically?

598. Have Digital Content Management project success criteria been defined?

599. Were escalated issues resolved promptly?

600. Who is involved?

601. Have Digital Content Management project team accountabilities & responsibilities been clearly defined?

602. Have all unresolved risks been documented?

603. Quality of people required to meet the forecast needs of the department?

604. Digital Content Management project definition & scope?

605. Is a pmo (Digital Content Management project management office) in place and provide oversight to the Digital Content Management project?

606. Are parking lot items captured?

607. Is this Digital Content Management project carried out in partnership with other groups/ organizations?

608. Was the Digital Content Management project schedule reviewed by all stakeholders and formally accepted?

609. What is this Digital Content Management project aiming to achieve?

610. Are status reports received per the Digital Content Management project Plan?

611. Are cause and effect determined for risks when others occur?

612. Did the Digital Content Management project team have the right skills?

2.30 Communications Management Plan: Digital Content Management

613. What to know?

614. Who is involved as you identify stakeholders?

615. What does the stakeholder need from the team?

616. How were corresponding initiatives successful?

617. In your work, how much time is spent on stakeholder identification?

618. Do you then often overlook a key stakeholder or stakeholder group?

619. Are there potential barriers between the team and the stakeholder?

620. What is the stakeholders level of authority?

621. How much time does it take to do it?

622. Who is the stakeholder?

623. Which stakeholders are thought leaders, influences, or early adopters?

624. Who will use or be affected by the result of a Digital Content Management project?

625. What approaches to you feel are the best ones to

use?

626. Who to learn from?

627. How is this initiative related to other portfolios, programs, or Digital Content Management projects?

628. Are there common objectives between the team and the stakeholder?

629. Who did you turn to if you had questions?

630. Are stakeholders internal or external?

631. Who needs to know and how much?

632. Do you prepare stakeholder engagement plans?

2.31 Risk Management Plan: Digital Content Management

633. Are enough people available?

634. Are there risks to human health or the environment that need to be controlled or mitigated?

635. Is the customer technically sophisticated in the product area?

636. What are it-specific requirements?

637. What is the likelihood that your organization would accept responsibility for the risk?

638. Do the people have the right combinations of skills?

639. Have top software and customer managers formally committed to support the Digital Content Management project?

640. What would you do differently?

641. Where do risks appear in the business phases?

642. Was an original risk assessment/risk management plan completed?

643. Financial risk -can your organization afford to undertake the Digital Content Management project?

644. How is risk monitoring performed?

645. Litigation – what is the probability that lawsuits will cause problems or delays in the Digital Content Management project?

646. Are tools for analysis and design available?

647. What are the chances the risk event will occur?

648. Are formal technical reviews part of this process?

649. Are tool mentors available?

650. Are Digital Content Management project requirements stable?

651. Are there alternative opinions/solutions/ processes you should explore?

652. Does the Digital Content Management project have the authority and ability to avoid the risk?

2.32 Risk Register: Digital Content Management

653. What could prevent you delivering on the strategic program objectives and what is being done to mitigate corresponding issues?

654. Assume the risk event or situation happens, what would the impact be?

655. What is a Risk?

656. How are risks graded?

657. When is it going to be done?

658. Why would you develop a risk register?

659. What are you going to do to limit the Digital Content Management projects risk exposure due to the identified risks?

660. Who is accountable?

661. What are the assumptions and current status that support the assessment of the risk?

662. Who is going to do it?

663. Schedule impact/severity estimated range (workdays) assume the event happens, what is the potential impact?

664. What can be done about it?

665. Are there any knock-on effects/impact on any of the other areas?

666. Methodology: how will risk management be performed on this Digital Content Management project?

667. What has changed since the last period?

668. Market risk -will the new service or product be useful to your organization or marketable to others?

669. User involvement: do you have the right users?

670. What is the appropriate level of risk management for this Digital Content Management project?

2.33 Probability and Impact Assessment: Digital Content Management

671. Can you avoid altogether some things that might go wrong?

672. Do you manage the process through use of metrics?

673. Are flexibility and reuse paramount?

674. Risk urgency assessment -which of your risks could occur soon, or require a longer planning time?

675. Will new information become available during the Digital Content Management project?

676. Monitoring of the overall Digital Content Management project status – are there any changes in the Digital Content Management project that can effect and cause new possible risks?

677. Are people attending meetings and doing work?

678. Prioritized components/features?

679. What are its business ethics?

680. What are the probabilities of chosen technologies being suitable for local conditions?

681. What should be the gestation period for the

Digital Content Management project with specific technology?

682. Are the risk data timely and relevant?

683. Have customers been involved fully in the definition of requirements?

684. Do you use diagramming techniques to show cause and effect?

685. What significant shift will occur in governmental policies, laws, and regulations pertaining to specific industries?

686. Is a software Digital Content Management project management tool available?

687. What risks are necessary to achieve success?

688. Are trained personnel, including supervisors and Digital Content Management project managers, available to handle such a large Digital Content Management project?

689. Are some people working on multiple Digital Content Management projects?

690. Do requirements put excessive performance constraints on the product?

2.34 Probability and Impact Matrix: Digital Content Management

691. What can you use the analyzed risks for?

692. Brain storm – mind maps, what if?

693. What are the likely future requirements?

694. To what extent is the chosen technology maturing?

695. What will be the environmental impact of the Digital Content Management project?

696. What should be done with risks on the watch list?

697. How would you suggest monitoring for risk transition indicators?

698. If you can not fix it, how do you do it differently?

699. What are the methods to deal with risks?

700. Is the customer willing to establish rapid communication links with the developer?

701. What should be the level of coordination?

702. Mandated specific features?

703. Have you ascribed a level of confidence to every critical technical objective?

704. Several experts are offsite, and wish to be included. How can this be done?

705. Is Digital Content Management project scope stable?

706. What can possibly go wrong?

2.35 Risk Data Sheet: Digital Content Management

707. Has a sensitivity analysis been carried out?

708. Type of risk identified?

709. How can hazards be reduced?

710. What if client refuses?

711. What can you do?

712. During work activities could hazards exist?

713. Who has a vested interest in how you perform as your organization (our stakeholders)?

714. Risk of what?

715. How can it happen?

716. What are the main opportunities available to you that you should grab while you can?

717. What are your core values?

718. Potential for recurrence?

719. Whom do you serve (customers)?

720. What can happen?

721. What are you trying to achieve (Objectives)?

722. What do people affected think about the need for, and practicality of preventive measures?

723. What is the environment within which you operate (social trends, economic, community values, broad based participation, national directions etc.)?

724. What actions can be taken to eliminate or remove risk?

725. What is the chance that it will happen?

2.36 Procurement Management Plan: Digital Content Management

726. Does the business case include how the Digital Content Management project aligns with your organizations strategic goals & objectives?

727. Do all stakeholders know how to access the PM repository and where to find the Digital Content Management project documentation?

728. Have key stakeholders been identified?

729. How will multiple providers be managed?

730. Have adequate resources been provided by management to ensure Digital Content Management project success?

731. If independent estimates will be needed as evaluation criteria, who will prepare them and when?

732. Does the resource management plan include a personnel development plan?

733. Have all documents been archived in a Digital Content Management project repository for each release?

734. Alignment to strategic goals & objectives?

735. What is the last item a Digital Content Management project manager must do to finalize

Digital Content Management project close-out?

736. Has the budget been baselined?

737. Are change requests logged and managed?

738. Specific - is the objective clear in terms of what, how, when, and where the situation will be changed?

739. Has the scope management document been updated and distributed to help prevent scope creep?

740. Is the Digital Content Management project sponsor clearly communicating the business case or rationale for why this Digital Content Management project is needed?

741. What communication items need improvement?

2.37 Source Selection Criteria: Digital Content Management

742. How much weight should be placed on past performance information?

743. How much past performance information should be requested?

744. Is this a cost contract?

745. How can solicitation Schedules be improved to yield more effective price competition?

746. What should be considered when developing evaluation standards?

747. With the rapid changes in information technology, will media be readable in five or ten years?

748. What source selection software is your team using?

749. How can the methods of publicizing the buy be tailored to yield more effective price competition?

750. Does the evaluation of any change include an impact analysis; how will the change affect the scope, time, cost, and quality of the goods or services being provided?

751. Do you ensure you evaluate what you asked for,

not what you want to see or expect to see?

752. What does an evaluation address and what does a sample resemble?

753. How is past performance evaluated?

754. What is price analysis and when should it be performed?

755. How and when do you enter into Digital Content Management project Procurement Management?

756. Do proposed hours support content and schedule?

757. In the technical/management area, what criteria do you use to determine the final evaluation ratings?

758. What can not be disclosed?

759. What is the last item a Digital Content Management project manager must do to finalize Digital Content Management project close-out?

760. Is there collaboration among your evaluators?

761. Are responses to considerations adequate?

2.38 Stakeholder Management Plan: Digital Content Management

762. Are metrics used to evaluate and manage Vendors?

763. Who would sign off on the charter?

764. Does the Digital Content Management project have a formal Digital Content Management project Plan?

765. Is there any form of automated support for Issues Management?

766. Is the assigned Digital Content Management project manager a PMP (Certified Digital Content Management project manager) and experienced?

767. Are communication systems proposed compatible with staff skills and experience?

768. Is the current scope of the Digital Content Management project substantially different than that originally defined?

769. What are the criteria for selecting suppliers of off the shelf products?

770. Do Digital Content Management project teams & team members report on status / activities / progress?

771. Have activity relationships and

interdependencies within tasks been adequately identified?

772. Are meeting objectives identified for each meeting?

773. Are Digital Content Management project leaders committed to this Digital Content Management project full time?

774. Will Digital Content Management project success require up to date information at a moments notice?

775. Have external dependencies been captured in the schedule?

776. Is the quality assurance team identified?

777. Are the people assigned to the Digital Content Management project sufficiently qualified?

778. What conditions make using three-point estimating justifiable?

2.39 Change Management Plan: Digital Content Management

779. What are the major changes to processes?

780. Has this been negotiated with the customer and sponsor?

781. How do you gain sponsors buy-in to the communication plan?

782. Are work location changes required?

783. What communication network would you use – informal or formal?

784. What are you trying to achieve as a result of communication?

785. What is going to be done differently?

786. Will you need new processes?

787. What new behaviours are required?

788. What policies and procedures need to be changed?

789. Will a different work structure focus people on what is important?

790. What are the specific target groups / audience that will be impacted by this change?

791. Has the relevant business unit been notified of installation and support requirements?

792. Does this change represent a completely new process for your organization, or a different application of an existing process?

793. What provokes organizational change?

794. What are the needs, priorities and special interests of the audience?

795. Has the priority for this Digital Content Management project been set by the Business Unit Management Team?

796. Has an information & communications plan been developed?

3.0 Executing Process Group: Digital Content Management

797. What are the challenges Digital Content Management project teams face?

798. Is the Digital Content Management project making progress in helping to achieve the set results?

799. When is the appropriate time to bring the scorecard to Board meetings?

800. How can software assist in Digital Content Management project communications?

801. Does software appear easy to learn?

802. How is Digital Content Management project performance information created and distributed?

803. Do the products created live up to the necessary quality?

804. How can your organization use a weighted decision matrix to evaluate proposals as part of source selection?

805. What is the difference between conceptual, application, and evaluative questions?

806. What were things that you did very well and want to do the same again on the next Digital Content Management project?

807. Do schedule issues conflicts?

808. How do you enter durations, link tasks, and view critical path information?

809. What does it mean to take a systems view of a Digital Content Management project?

810. If action is called for, what form should it take?

811. Does the Digital Content Management project team have enough people to execute the Digital Content Management project plan?

812. Do your results resemble a normal distribution?

813. Were sponsors and decision makers available when needed outside regularly scheduled meetings?

814. Are the necessary foundations in place to ensure the sustainability of the results of the programme?

3.1 Team Member Status Report: Digital Content Management

815. What specific interest groups do you have in place?

816. Is there evidence that staff is taking a more professional approach toward management of your organizations Digital Content Management projects?

817. Are the attitudes of staff regarding Digital Content Management project work improving?

818. Are your organizations Digital Content Management projects more successful over time?

819. How much risk is involved?

820. Will the staff do training or is that done by a third party?

821. Do you have an Enterprise Digital Content Management project Management Office (EPMO)?

822. How will resource planning be done?

823. How it is to be done?

824. Does every department have to have a Digital Content Management project Manager on staff?

825. Why is it to be done?

826. When a teams productivity and success depend on collaboration and the efficient flow of information, what generally fails them?

827. The problem with Reward & Recognition Programs is that the truly deserving people all too often get left out. How can you make it practical?

828. Are the products of your organizations Digital Content Management projects meeting customers objectives?

829. How does this product, good, or service meet the needs of the Digital Content Management project and your organization as a whole?

830. How can you make it practical?

831. Does the product, good, or service already exist within your organization?

832. What is to be done?

833. Does your organization have the means (staff, money, contract, etc.) to produce or to acquire the product, good, or service?

3.2 Change Request: Digital Content Management

834. How is the change documented (format, content, storage)?

835. Are there requirements attributes that are strongly related to the complexity and size?

836. How many times must the change be modified or presented to the change control board before it is approved?

837. What is the relationship between requirements attributes and attributes like complexity and size?

838. What are the requirements for urgent changes?

839. Is it feasible to use requirements attributes as predictors of reliability?

840. Why control change across the life cycle?

841. What are the duties of the change control team?

842. Has a formal technical review been conducted to assess technical correctness?

843. Has your address changed?

844. Have scm procedures for noting the change, recording it, and reporting it been followed?

845. What needs to be communicated?

846. Who can suggest changes?

847. Screen shots or attachments included in a Change Request?

848. Why do you want to have a change control system?

849. Where do changes come from?

850. Are you implementing itil processes?

851. Who is communicating the change?

852. What mechanism is used to appraise others of changes that are made?

853. How does a team identify the discrete elements of a configuration?

3.3 Change Log: Digital Content Management

854. How does this relate to the standards developed for specific business processes?

855. Is the change request open, closed or pending?

856. Does the suggested change request represent a desired enhancement to the products functionality?

857. Who initiated the change request?

858. Do the described changes impact on the integrity or security of the system?

859. How does this change affect the timeline of the schedule?

860. Will the Digital Content Management project fail if the change request is not executed?

861. How does this change affect scope?

862. Is the change request within Digital Content Management project scope?

863. Is this a mandatory replacement?

864. When was the request submitted?

865. Is the requested change request a result of changes in other Digital Content Management

project(s)?

866. When was the request approved?

867. Is the change backward compatible without limitations?

868. Is the submitted change a new change or a modification of a previously approved change?

3.4 Decision Log: Digital Content Management

869. It becomes critical to track and periodically revisit both operational effectiveness; Are you noticing all that you need to, and are you interpreting what you see effectively?

870. How do you define success?

871. Who will be given a copy of this document and where will it be kept?

872. Decision-making process; how will the team make decisions?

873. Do strategies and tactics aimed at less than full control reduce the costs of management or simply shift the cost burden?

874. What is the average size of your matters in an applicable measurement?

875. Which variables make a critical difference?

876. Who is the decisionmaker?

877. How does provision of information, both in terms of content and presentation, influence acceptance of alternative strategies?

878. Behaviors; what are guidelines that the team has identified that will assist them with getting the most

out of team meetings?

879. Is your opponent open to a non-traditional workflow, or will it likely challenge anything you do?

880. Meeting purpose; why does this team meet?

881. What alternatives/risks were considered?

882. How does an increasing emphasis on cost containment influence the strategies and tactics used?

883. What is the line where eDiscovery ends and document review begins?

884. What makes you different or better than others companies selling the same thing?

885. How effective is maintaining the log at facilitating organizational learning?

886. What is your overall strategy for quality control / quality assurance procedures?

887. Is everything working as expected?

888. At what point in time does loss become unacceptable?

3.5 Quality Audit: Digital Content Management

889. How does your organization know that the range and quality of its accommodation, catering and transportation services are appropriately effective and constructive?

890. How does the organization know that its industry and community engagement planning and management systems are appropriately effective and constructive in enabling relationships with key stakeholder groups?

891. Is there any content that may be legally actionable?

892. How does your organization know that the support for its staff is appropriately effective and constructive?

893. Do prior clients have a positive opinion of your organization?

894. How does your organization know that its public relations and marketing systems are appropriately effective and constructive?

895. How does your organization know that it provides a safe and healthy environment?

896. What is the collective experience of the team to be assigned to an audit?

897. Are all employees made aware of device defects which may occur from the improper performance of specific jobs?

898. Are all complaints involving the possible failure of a device, labeling, or packaging to meet any of its specifications reviewed, evaluated, and investigated?

899. How does your organization know that its system for attending to the particular needs of its international staff is appropriately effective and constructive?

900. How does your organization know that it is effectively and constructively guiding staff through to timely completion of tasks?

901. How does your organization know that its system for managing intellectual property issues is appropriately effective, constructive and fair?

902. How does your organization know that its staff embody the core knowledge, skills and characteristics for which it wishes to be recognized?

903. How does your organization know that its systems for meeting staff extracurricular learning support requirements are appropriately effective and constructive?

904. Do the suppliers use a formal quality system?

905. How does your organization know that its advisory services are appropriately effective and constructive?

906. How does your organization know that its system for supporting staff research capability is appropriately effective and constructive?

907. How does your organization know that its system for governing staff behaviour is appropriately effective and constructive?

908. How are you auditing your organizations compliance with regulations?

3.6 Team Directory: Digital Content Management

909. How will the team handle changes?

910. Who will write the meeting minutes and distribute?

911. Process decisions: is work progressing on schedule and per contract requirements?

912. When will you produce deliverables?

913. When does information need to be distributed?

914. Who are the Team Members?

915. Have you decided when to celebrate the Digital Content Management projects completion date?

916. How does the team resolve conflicts and ensure tasks are completed?

917. Process decisions: which organizational elements and which individuals will be assigned management functions?

918. Does a Digital Content Management project team directory list all resources assigned to the Digital Content Management project?

919. What are you going to deliver or accomplish?

920. Who should receive information (all stakeholders)?

921. Do purchase specifications and configurations match requirements?

922. How do unidentified risks impact the outcome of the Digital Content Management project?

923. How and in what format should information be presented?

924. Why is the work necessary?

925. Process decisions: are contractors adequately prosecuting the work?

926. Where will the product be used and/or delivered or built when appropriate?

927. Decisions: is the most suitable form of contract being used?

928. Process decisions: how well was task order work performed?

3.7 Team Operating Agreement: Digital Content Management

929. What are the boundaries (organizational or geographic) within which you operate?

930. Do you listen for voice tone and word choice to understand the meaning behind words?

931. Are there the right people on your team?

932. Did you prepare participants for the next meeting?

933. What is group supervision?

934. Do you ensure that all participants know how to use the required technology?

935. What are some potential sources of conflict among team members?

936. The method to be used in the decision making process; Will it be consensus, majority rule, or the supervisor having the final say?

937. Do you post meeting notes and the recording (if used) and notify participants?

938. Do you record meetings for the already stated unable to attend?

939. Do you ask participants to close laptops and

place mobile devices on silent on the table while the meeting is in progress?

940. Communication protocols: how will the team communicate?

941. What is culture?

942. How do you want to be thought of and known within your organization?

943. How will group handle unplanned absences?

944. Did you draft the meeting agenda?

945. Does your team need access to all documents and information at all times?

946. Are there more than two national cultures represented by your team?

947. Do you use a parking lot for any items that are important and outside of the agenda?

948. Reimbursements: how will the team members be reimbursed for expenses and time commitments?

3.8 Team Performance Assessment: Digital Content Management

949. What makes opportunities more or less obvious?

950. How does Digital Content Management project termination impact Digital Content Management project team members?

951. Does more radicalness mean more perceived benefits?

952. What are teams?

953. To what degree do team members articulate the teams work approach?

954. To what degree are the members clear on what they are individually responsible for and what they are jointly responsible for?

955. Lack of method variance in self-reported affect and perceptions at work: Reality or artifact?

956. Can team performance be reliably measured in simulator and live exercises using the same assessment tool?

957. To what degree do team members feel that the purpose of the team is important, if not exciting?

958. To what degree do team members frequently explore the teams purpose and its implications?

959. To what degree does the teams purpose constitute a broader, deeper aspiration than just accomplishing short-term goals?

960. To what degree are staff involved as partners in the improvement process?

961. To what degree will team members, individually and collectively, commit time to help themselves and others learn and develop skills?

962. What structural changes have you made or are you preparing to make?

963. To what degree can the team ensure that all members are individually and jointly accountable for the teams purpose, goals, approach, and work-products?

964. To what degree does the teams purpose contain themes that are particularly meaningful and memorable?

965. To what degree does the team possess adequate membership to achieve its ends?

966. To what degree does the teams approach to its work allow for modification and improvement over time?

967. How do you keep key people outside the group informed about its accomplishments?

968. How do you encourage members to learn from each other?

3.9 Team Member Performance Assessment: Digital Content Management

969. What are acceptable governance changes?

970. How often should assessments be conducted?

971. What stakeholders must be involved in the development and oversight of the performance plan?

972. What are the evaluation strategies (e.g., reaction, learning, behavior, results) used. What evaluation results did you have?

973. To what degree is the team cognizant of small wins to be celebrated along the way?

974. What variables that affect team members achievement are within your control?

975. How do you create a self-sustaining capacity for a collaborative culture?

976. How is assessment information achieved, stored?

977. How will you identify your Team Leaders?

978. To what degree are the skill areas critical to team performance present?

979. Are any validation activities performed?

980. How does your team work together?

981. Does the rater (supervisor) have the authority or responsibility to tell an employee that the employees performance is unsatisfactory?

982. To what degree can team members meet frequently enough to accomplish the teams ends?

983. What are the staffs preferences for training on technology-based platforms?

984. Why do performance reviews?

985. How do you use data to inform instruction and improve staff achievement?

986. Does the rater (supervisor) have to wait for the interim or final performance assessment review to tell an employee that the employees performance is unsatisfactory?

987. Are assessment validation activities performed?

3.10 Issue Log: Digital Content Management

988. How often do you engage with stakeholders?

989. What are the typical contents?

990. Where do team members get information?

991. Is access to the Issue Log controlled?

992. Who reported the issue?

993. Who were proponents/opponents?

994. Are stakeholder roles recognized by your organization?

995. Who have you worked with in past, similar initiatives?

996. What is a change?

997. How were past initiatives successful?

998. How do you manage human resources?

999. Who is the issue assigned to?

1000. Is the issue log kept in a safe place?

4.0 Monitoring and Controlling Process Group: Digital Content Management

1001. What resources are necessary?

1002. Are the services being delivered?

1003. What are the goals of the program?

1004. What do they need to know about the Digital Content Management project?

1005. Is there adequate validation on required fields?

1006. What input will you be required to provide the Digital Content Management project team?

1007. Who needs to be involved in the planning?

1008. How many more potential communications channels were introduced by the discovery of the new stakeholders?

1009. Accuracy: what design will lead to accurate information?

1010. Does the solution fit in with organizations technical architectural requirements?

1011. Where is the Risk in the Digital Content Management project?

1012. If a risk event occurs, what will you do?

1013. Where is the Risk in the Digital Content Management project?

1014. Did you implement the program as designed?

1015. Contingency planning. if a risk event occurs, what will you do?

1016. How to ensure validity, quality and consistency?

1017. How well defined and documented were the Digital Content Management project management processes you chose to use?

4.1 Project Performance Report: Digital Content Management

1018. To what degree does the teams work approach provide opportunity for members to engage in fact-based problem solving?

1019. To what degree do all members feel responsible for all agreed-upon measures?

1020. To what degree does the task meet individual needs?

1021. To what degree does the teams work approach provide opportunity for members to engage in open interaction?

1022. To what degree is there centralized control of information sharing?

1023. To what degree are the goals realistic?

1024. To what degree can all members engage in open and interactive considerations?

1025. What is the degree to which rules govern information exchange between individuals within your organization?

1026. To what degree does the formal organization make use of individual resources and meet individual needs?

1027. What is the PRS?

1028. To what degree do members articulate the goals beyond the team membership?

1029. To what degree will each member have the opportunity to advance his or her professional skills in all three of the above categories while contributing to the accomplishment of the teams purpose and goals?

1030. To what degree are the teams goals and objectives clear, simple, and measurable?

4.2 Variance Analysis: Digital Content Management

1031. When, during the last four quarters, did a primary business event occur causing a fluctuation?

1032. Does the scheduling system identify in a timely manner the status of work?

1033. How does your organization measure performance?

1034. Are estimates of costs at completion generated in a rational, consistent manner?

1035. Can the contractor substantiate work package and planning package budgets?

1036. Does the contractor use objective results, design reviews and tests to trace schedule performance?

1037. Are the requirements for all items of overhead established by rational, traceable processes?

1038. Are records maintained to show how undistributed budgets are controlled?

1039. Is work progressively subdivided into detailed work packages as requirements are defined?

1040. Do work packages consist of discrete tasks which are adequately described?

1041. Are there changes in the direct base to which overhead costs are allocated?

1042. Are indirect costs accumulated for comparison with the corresponding budgets?

1043. Are significant decision points, constraints, and interfaces identified as key milestones?

1044. Are authorized changes being incorporated in a timely manner?

1045. Are indirect costs charged to the appropriate indirect pools and incurring organization?

1046. Does the accounting system provide a basis for auditing records of direct costs chargeable to the contract?

1047. How does the use of a single conversion element (rather than the traditional labor and overhead elements) affect standard costing?

1048. The anticipated business volume?

1049. Other relevant issues of Variance Analysis -selling price or gross margin?

4.3 Earned Value Status: Digital Content Management

1050. Earned value can be used in almost any Digital Content Management project situation and in almost any Digital Content Management project environment. it may be used on large Digital Content Management projects, medium sized Digital Content Management projects, tiny Digital Content Management projects (in cut-down form), complex and simple Digital Content Management projects and in any market sector. some people, of course, know all about earned value, they have used it for years - but perhaps not as effectively as they could have?

1051. Validation is a process of ensuring that the developed system will actually achieve the stakeholders desired outcomes; Are you building the right product? What do you validate?

1052. How does this compare with other Digital Content Management projects?

1053. When is it going to finish?

1054. Are you hitting your Digital Content Management projects targets?

1055. Verification is a process of ensuring that the developed system satisfies the stakeholders agreements and specifications; Are you building the product right? What do you verify?

1056. How much is it going to cost by the finish?

1057. Where are your problem areas?

1058. If earned value management (EVM) is so good in determining the true status of a Digital Content Management project and Digital Content Management project its completion, why is it that hardly any one uses it in information systems related Digital Content Management projects?

1059. Where is evidence-based earned value in your organization reported?

1060. What is the unit of forecast value?

4.4 Risk Audit: Digital Content Management

1061. Are auditors able to effectively apply more soft evidence found in the risk-assessment process with the results of more tangible audit evidence found through more substantive testing?

1062. To what extent are auditors influenced by the business risk assessment in the audit process, and how can auditors create more effective mental models to more fully examine contradictory evidence?

1063. Is your organization willing to commit significant time to the requirements gathering process?

1064. From an empirical perspective, does the business risk approach lead to a more effective audit, or simply to increased consulting revenue detrimental to audit rigor?

1065. Do you have a clear plan for the future that describes what you want to do and how you are going to do it?

1066. Have you reviewed your constitution within the last twelve months?

1067. To what extent should analytical procedures be utilized in the risk-assessment process?

1068. Does your board meet regularly and document all decisions and actions?

1069. What programmatic and Fiscal information is being collected and analyzed?

1070. Do you have proper induction processes for all new paid staff and volunteers who have a specific role and responsibility?

1071. What is the effect of globalisation; is business becoming too complex and can the auditor rely on auditing standards?

1072. Does willful intent modify risk-based auditing?

1073. If applicable; which route/packaging option do you choose for transport of hazmat material?

1074. To what extent are auditors effective at linking business risks and management assertions?

1075. For this risk .. what do you need to stop doing, start doing and keep doing?

1076. Who is responsible for what?

1077. Is there a screening process that will ensure all participants have the fitness and skills required to safely participate?

1078. Assessing risk with analytical procedures: do systemsthinking tools help auditors focus on diagnostic patterns?

4.5 Contractor Status Report: Digital Content Management

1079. What was the final actual cost?

1080. How is risk transferred?

1081. If applicable; describe your standard schedule for new software version releases. Are new software version releases included in the standard maintenance plan?

1082. What process manages the contracts?

1083. What was the actual budget or estimated cost for your organizations services?

1084. Who can list a Digital Content Management project as organization experience, your organization or a previous employee of your organization?

1085. What is the average response time for answering a support call?

1086. What was the overall budget or estimated cost?

1087. Are there contractual transfer concerns?

1088. Describe how often regular updates are made to the proposed solution. Are corresponding regular updates included in the standard maintenance plan?

1089. How does the proposed individual meet each

requirement?

1090. What was the budget or estimated cost for your organizations services?

1091. How long have you been using the services?

1092. What are the minimum and optimal bandwidth requirements for the proposed solution?

4.6 Formal Acceptance: Digital Content Management

1093. What was done right?

1094. General estimate of the costs and times to complete the Digital Content Management project?

1095. Does it do what client said it would?

1096. Who would use it?

1097. Was business value realized?

1098. What function(s) does it fill or meet?

1099. What features, practices, and processes proved to be strengths or weaknesses?

1100. Was the Digital Content Management project goal achieved?

1101. Who supplies data?

1102. Was the Digital Content Management project work done on time, within budget, and according to specification?

1103. What is the Acceptance Management Process?

1104. What can you do better next time?

1105. Do you perform formal acceptance or burn-in

tests?

1106. Do you buy pre-configured systems or build your own configuration?

1107. Is formal acceptance of the Digital Content Management project product documented and distributed?

1108. What are the requirements against which to test, Who will execute?

1109. Do you buy-in installation services?

1110. What lessons were learned about your Digital Content Management project management methodology?

1111. How well did the team follow the methodology?

1112. Was the sponsor/customer satisfied?

5.0 Closing Process Group: Digital Content Management

1113. How well did you do?

1114. Can the lesson learned be replicated?

1115. Are there funding or time constraints?

1116. What areas were overlooked on this Digital Content Management project?

1117. Were the outcomes different from the already stated planned?

1118. What is the amount of funding and what Digital Content Management project phases are funded?

1119. Is the Digital Content Management project funded?

1120. What could have been improved?

1121. Who are the Digital Content Management project stakeholders?

1122. What was learned?

1123. Did you do things well?

1124. How well did the chosen processes fit the needs of the Digital Content Management project?

5.1 Procurement Audit: Digital Content Management

1125. Did the chosen procedure ensure fair competition and transparency?

1126. Are vendor price lists regularly updated?

1127. Did your organization identify the full contract value and include options and provisions for renewals?

1128. Were calculations used in evaluation adequate and correct?

1129. Does procurement staff have recognized professional procurement qualifications or sufficient training?

1130. Has the department identified and described the different elements in the procurement process?

1131. Are risks managed to provide reasonable assurance regarding department procurement objectives?

1132. Is there a legal authority for the procurement Digital Content Management project?

1133. Are the established budget and timetable (milestones) respected?

1134. Was the estimated contract value based on

realistic and updated prices?

1135. Do the buyers always select or authorize the source of supply on other than contract purchases?

1136. Did your organization state the minimum requirements to be met by the variants in the tender documents?

1137. Have late payment interests been rewarded and could they have been avoided?

1138. Does the individual approving disbursements sign or initial the document?

1139. If a purchase order calls for a cost-plus agreement, is the method of determining how final charges will be determined specified?

1140. Were there no material changes in the contract shortly after award?

1141. Does each policy statement contain the legal reference(s) on which the policy is based?

1142. Has the expected benefits from realisation of the procurement Digital Content Management project been calculated?

1143. Are all checks stored in a secure area?

1144. Was timely and equal access to contract documents and information provided to all candidates?

5.2 Contract Close-Out: Digital Content Management

1145. Change in circumstances?

1146. Was the contract sufficiently clear so as not to result in numerous disputes and misunderstandings?

1147. What happens to the recipient of services?

1148. Has each contract been audited to verify acceptance and delivery?

1149. What is capture management?

1150. Have all contract records been included in the Digital Content Management project archives?

1151. Parties: Authorized?

1152. Are the signers the authorized officials?

1153. How does it work?

1154. Change in attitude or behavior?

1155. Was the contract complete without requiring numerous changes and revisions?

1156. How is the contracting office notified of the automatic contract close-out?

1157. Parties: who is involved?

1158. Have all contracts been completed?

1159. Why Outsource?

1160. Was the contract type appropriate?

1161. Have all contracts been closed?

1162. Change in knowledge?

1163. How/when used ?

1164. Have all acceptance criteria been met prior to final payment to contractors?

5.3 Project or Phase Close-Out: Digital Content Management

1165. How much influence did the stakeholder have over others?

1166. What was expected from each stakeholder?

1167. Is the lesson significant, valid, and applicable?

1168. Who controlled key decisions that were made?

1169. When and how were information needs best met?

1170. What stakeholder group needs, expectations, and interests are being met by the Digital Content Management project?

1171. Were messages directly related to the release strategy or phases of the Digital Content Management project?

1172. What information is each stakeholder group interested in?

1173. What were the goals and objectives of the communications strategy for the Digital Content Management project?

1174. What is this stakeholder expecting?

1175. Is there a clear cause and effect between the

activity and the lesson learned?

1176. If you were the Digital Content Management project sponsor, how would you determine which Digital Content Management project team(s) and/or individuals deserve recognition?

1177. Was the user/client satisfied with the end product?

1178. Was the schedule met?

1179. Who controlled the resources for the Digital Content Management project?

1180. What can you do better next time, and what specific actions can you take to improve?

1181. What are the mandatory communication needs for each stakeholder?

1182. Did the delivered product meet the specified requirements and goals of the Digital Content Management project?

5.4 Lessons Learned: Digital Content Management

1183. What rewards do the individuals seek?

1184. How effective were your design reviews?

1185. What is the frequency of communication?

1186. Who needs to learn lessons?

1187. How satisfied are you with your involvement in the development and/or review of the Digital Content Management project Scope during Digital Content Management project Initiation and Planning?

1188. What policy constraints are relevant?

1189. Were any strategies or activities unsuccessful?

1190. What report generation capability is needed?

1191. What is the proportion of in-house and contractor personnel authorized for the Digital Content Management project?

1192. Were risks identified and mitigated?

1193. How well were Digital Content Management project issues communicated throughout your involvement in the Digital Content Management project?

1194. What are the funding priorities for intelligence?

1195. How much communication is socially oriented?

1196. What is in the future?

1197. How many interest groups are stakeholders?

1198. Are lessons learned documented?

1199. Is your organization willing to expose problems or mistakes for the betterment of the collective whole, and can you do this in a way that does not intimidate employees or workers?

1200. What were the major enablers to a quick response?

1201. Was there enough support – guidance, clerical support, training?

Index

Digital 1-14, 16-90, 92-102, 104-117, 119-136, 138-148, 150-154, 156-157, 159-163, 165-180, 182-186, 188, 190, 192-208, 210-222, 224, 226, 228, 231-233, 235, 237, 239-242, 244, 246-248, 250, 252-257, 259-261

dilemma   128
dimensions   25
direct 112, 156, 192, 245
direction   40, 50, 141
directions   209
directly 1, 59, 69, 259
Directory   6, 231
Disagree   11, 16, 28, 44, 59, 75, 91, 103
disaster   57, 64
discarded   153
disclosed   213
disclosure   101
discovery   240
discrete   223, 244
display 166
displayed   42, 62, 161, 174
disputes   257
disqualify   64
disruptive   60
distribute   231
Divided   27, 35, 43, 58, 74, 90, 102, 129
division 140
document   10, 31, 87, 140, 146, 152-153, 211, 226-227, 249, 256
documented 39, 83, 87, 95-96, 98-99, 150, 152-153, 157, 184-185, 195-196, 222, 241, 253, 262
documents   8, 77, 81, 85, 150, 152, 172, 188, 210, 234, 256
dollars 157, 192
dormant   115
Driver 72
drivers 51, 61
drives 52
driving 111
Duration   4, 138, 167, 172, 174
durations   34, 219
during 40, 88, 132, 141, 143, 159, 169, 204, 208, 244, 261
duties 222
dynamic   56
dynamics   30

reported   144, 189, 239, 247
reporting   60, 98, 108, 145, 188, 222
reports 55, 97, 135, 145, 196-197
repository   210
represent   82, 184, 217, 224
reproduced   1
reputation   117
request   6, 69, 145, 184-185, 222-225
requested   1, 82, 212, 224
requests   211
require 36, 52, 60, 99, 169, 204, 215
required   17, 20, 28, 31-32, 36-38, 47, 54, 69, 76, 80, 84, 145,
147, 153, 162-164, 174, 189, 191, 193, 195-196, 216, 233, 240, 249
requiring   135, 257
research   23, 100, 118, 230
resemble   213, 219
Reserve   180
reserved   1
reserves   192
reside 87
resolution   67, 76, 151
resolve 20, 22, 231
resolved   196
Resource   4-5, 138, 159, 163, 169-171, 196, 210, 220
resources   2, 8, 17, 19-20, 25, 32, 35, 68, 76, 93, 111, 115,
121, 131, 136, 142, 150, 153, 160, 163-164, 167, 171, 182, 185,
210, 231, 239-240, 242, 260
respect   1
respected   255
respond   139
responded   12
response   18, 23, 92, 94, 96, 100, 118, 250, 262
responses   78, 104, 213
responsive   175, 182
result   82-83, 180, 183, 188, 198, 216, 224, 257
resulted   91
resulting   70, 141
results 9, 30, 34, 46, 59, 75, 78-80, 86, 88, 90, 95, 101, 132, 138-
140, 172, 178, 183, 186, 191, 218-219, 237, 244, 248
retain   103, 186-187
retained   71
retention   47, 85
retrospect   106

success   20-21, 30, 33, 38, 48-49, 78, 87, 106, 110-111, 119,
122, 124, 129, 133, 142, 150, 153, 167, 196, 205, 210, 215, 221,
226
successes   121
successful   79, 97, 134, 171, 184, 198, 220, 239
succession   91
sufficient   255
suggest   206, 223
suggested   99, 184, 224
suitable   204, 232
summarized   156
supervisor   194, 233, 238
supplier   83, 126
suppliers   34, 63, 124, 214, 229
supplies   252
supply 57, 165, 256
support   8, 19, 62, 78, 92-93, 97, 106, 113, 131-132, 156,
169, 200, 202, 213-214, 217, 228-229, 250, 262
supported   37, 72, 138
supporting   80, 101, 187, 230
supportive   195
surface   100
SUSTAIN   2, 77, 103
Sustaining   98, 166
symptom   16, 49
system 10, 23, 40, 62-63, 69, 73, 85, 87, 101, 105, 124, 146-147,
153, 156, 170, 192, 195, 223-224, 229-230, 244-246
systematic   53, 55
systems   55, 67, 71-73, 87-88, 92, 118, 214, 219, 228-229,
247, 253
tables 152
tackle 49
tactics 226-227
Taguchi   172
tailored   212
taking 50, 220
talent 66, 108
talking 8
tangible   248
target 30, 105, 112, 216
targets 107, 132, 246
tasked 96
taxable   64, 119

301

Made in United States
North Haven, CT
07 September 2022

23755659R00183